Transition to CADD

A Practical Guide for Architects,
Engineers, and Designers

Gary M. Gerlach

McGraw-Hill Book Company

New York St. Louis San Francisco Auckland Bogotá
Hamburg Johannesburg London Madrid Mexico
Milan Montreal New Delhi Panama
Paris São Paulo Singapore
Sydney Tokyo Toronto

Library of Congress Cataloging-in-Publication Data

Gerlach, Gary M.
  Transition to CADD.

  (The McGraw-Hill designing with systems series)
  Bibliography: p.
  Includes index.
  1. Computer-aided design. 2. Engineering design—
Data processing. 3. Architectural design—Data
processing. I. Title. II. Series.
TA174.G48   1987   620'.00425'0285   86-27802
ISBN   0-07-023072-2

1234567890   DOC/DOC   8932109876

ISBN 0-07-023072-2

*The editors for this book were Nadine M. Post and Georgia Kornbluth,
the designer was Naomi Auerbach, and the production
supervisor was Thomas G. Kowalczyk. It was set in Century Schoolbook
by Williams Press, Inc.*

Printed and bound by R. R. Donnelley & Sons Company.

Contents

Preface   vii

Chapter 1. CADD Systems Overview   1

   1.1   From Drafting to CADD Layering   2
   1.2   Data Logic and Graphics Logic   10
   1.3   Minimum Software and Hardware Packages   15

Chapter 2. CADD Acquisition Management   24

   2.1   Project Cost Controls   24
   2.2   Project Application Checklists   32
   2.3   Minimal Investment Package plus Upgrade   37
   2.4   Capital Investment versus Service Bureau   40
   2.5   Evaluation of Personnel Training Programs   41

Chapter 3. Design Process Impact: CADD Input Managing   43

   3.1   Design Process Impact Points   45
   3.2   Application Justification at Impact Points   60
   3.3   Percentage and Types of Drawings on the System   62
   3.4   Interface between System Language and Consultants   66

Chapter 4. Layering Logic Control   69

   4.1   Setup Rules and Examples of Project Drawings   72
   4.2   Graphics Layering Logic: Two-Dimensional and Three-Dimensional   76
   4.3   Graphics Layering Logic: Solids Modeling   83
   4.4   Graphics Layering Logic: Color   84
   4.5   Operator-Machine Interface   88

Chapter 5. Hardcopy Output Managing   92

   5.1   Input from the Output Standpoint   94
   5.2   Output Devices and Functions   100
   5.3   Generating Hardcopy Output   104
   5.4   Working with CADD Hardcopy Output   108

Chapter 6. Output Filing and Maintenance   **113**

6.1 Electronic Filing   115
6.2 Revising and Retrieving Electronic Output   121
6.3 Plot-File Maintenance   122
6.4 Hardcopy Filing   125
6.5 Revising and Retrieving Hardcopy Output   127

Chapter 7. Alternative Parallel Approaches   **131**

7.1 What to Do with What Is Not CADD   132
7.2 Mixing CADD with Conventional Drafting   136
7.3 Mixing CADD with Pin-Registered Overlays   141

Glossary   153
References   169
Index   173

Preface

Transition to CADD offers a methodology and procedure for the acquisition and use of computer systems for design and drafting. This book is primarily intended for use by individuals and committees whose design and drafting firms presently do not have computer systems but are looking into the prospect of acquiring them. It should also be useful for firms that want to achieve greater productivity with existing computer systems, specifically computer-aided design and drafting (CADD) systems.

This book is not intended for general computer systems or software design, nor as an operations manual for any specific computer system. What is included are general applications and suggestions for incorporating current standard design office production procedures. Enhanced design communication by the production of drawings using interactive graphic computer systems as an assistant to the designer and drafter is a goal of this book.

As an example for applying the recommendations in this book, consider a 10-person engineering, architectural, or industrial design firm which is about to purchase an interactive computer graphics system for one of its workstations. Which of the 10 conventional workstations shall this CADD system replace? Or is the CADD workstation to be an additional work area? Then too, what will be done with the remaining 9 (or 10) persons in the firm? Most important, how will the output from the CADD workstation be integrated with the manual output from the existing engineers, designers, and drafters?

Process Flow

The sequence of chapter themes closely parallels the normal design process:

CADD Systems Overview	▪ Project analysis
CADD Acquisition Management	▪ Start preliminaries, set manpower

Design Process Impact:	▪ Design development
CADD Input Managing	
Layering Logic Control	▪ Production process techniques
Hardcopy Output Managing	▪ Contract documents production
Output Filing and Maintenance	▪ File maintenance and retrieval
Alternative Parallel Approaches	▪ Reviewing production results

The logic theme starts in Chapter 1, CADD Systems Overview: if we are designing and drafting by hand today, what steps do we take to achieve full use of CADD assistance? All the rules, shortcuts, and production methods that we have learned over many years through classwork and then in professional offices need not be forgotten. Instead, they must be taught to the computer; they must be configured into the operating system and installed into the database.

Should the computer system be acquired as a design tool or as a drafting tool, or both (Chapter 2, CADD Acquisition Management)? Reversing the thrust of this logic, which project—actually which portions of a project—will be best served by a CADD workstation? Too often, in the heat of purchasing high-technology equipment, the specific applications are not clearly chosen and valuable time is lost in waiting for the proper project to catch up. Considering the end result of CADD first, before purchase or other acquisition, allows not only cost justification but also best-use application.

How does a CADD system impact upon the design process? In seeking an answer to this question, Chapter 3, Design Process Impact: CADD Input Managing, may rank as one of the most important chapters of this book. The various aspects of design analysis are considered as input to a CADD system for comprehensive review. The next consideration is what form the CADD output should take, from this initial process point, so that it will be acceptable for the next, or preliminary design, process step.

This input-work-output functional test is applied to each step in the design, then draft, then fabricate process. The computer is an aid to this design and drafting process. The computer requires input, both data and instructions, so that it can do its programmed work. The CADD system has not accomplished its task until it generates output, either display or softcopy or hardcopy—and this output must be useful for the succeeding step. If not, the CADD system can be deemed useless, misapplied, or a financial waste.

Working with a CADD system generally requires a thorough understanding of layering logic (Chapter 4, Layering Logic Control). The tree structure of computer software and filing methods can be likened to layers of data and instructions. Similarly, drawings created on the CADD system are composed of alphanumeric and graphic primitives which can be accumulated in a series of related electronic layers or files.

Manual drafting systems often utilize a series of physically registered layers to increase productivity and interchangeability. These physical layers could provide an excellent transition to a more productive use of CADD. The structured sharing of common data and images is fundamental to a CADD system. Even though Chapter 4 may not seem to be the most exciting part of the book, in it you will find some helpful insights and some methods for establishing shared drawing files.

Hardcopy Is the Output

If CADD is a design tool, show me its design displays. If CADD is a drafting tool, show me its drawing plots. Whether CADD is used for design or drafting, its output is paramount. Only by the output of CADD can we judge the value of CADD. And since design and drafting function primarily with physical drawings or images, it is generally through hardcopy output that CADD participates in the communication of a project's design (Chapter 5, Hardcopy Output Managing).

Referring back to the example of a 10-person office adding a CADD workstation, note that the only true test of how the CADD system would best fit in with the existing team would be how the plotted or printed reproductions of the electronic database would function alongside the manually created hardcopy. Of course, some companies may use the CADD system solely for one project or one portion of a project, and thus may not require that CADD hardcopy mesh with manual hardcopy. Then again, some firms may use a CADD system only as a marketing tool and not for production output.

One thing for sure is that a CADD system will create far more files at an incredibly faster rate than do manual systems (Chapter 6, Output Filing and Maintenance). More files means more requirements for proper document retrieval and storage. A primary aspect of CADD files, as softcopy (electromagnetic potentials) rather than as hardcopy, is that they can be easily lost or rendered invalid. Thus a practical system, or series of systems, must be established for output filing and maintenance. And in order to do it right, these filing procedures must be instituted before any CADD drawings or database structures are created.

Alternative Approaches

If not CADD, then what? Chapter 7, Alternative Parallel Approaches, deals in more depth with ways to mix CADD output with non-CADD design process output, and with the associated drafting output methods. Just as the 10-person design firm in our example must properly configure the CADD system and then incorporate the CADD output into the overall project output, this firm must also coordinate its unique CADD system with the CADD systems and input-output requirements of outside consultants. Further, the softcopy or hardcopy requirements of the clients or ultimate users of the project facilities or items may dictate not only the firm's output but possibly even the type of operating system required for its CADD system.

Again it must be said: consider the end result or output first, in order to get the most from your CADD system.

Acknowledgments

This book could not have been written without the myriad individuals, institutions, and companies that have allowed me opportunities to learn how to get output from a computer system. At the University of Michigan between 1961 and 1966, the course of architectural instruction included demands for understanding how to use and then design for the installation of computer systems.

At Skidmore, Owings & Merrill in Chicago in the late 1960s, the in-house computer programming courses introduced the fundamentals and then showed how preliminary design analysis could be enhanced with computers, thus impressing the client. Looking back, even then, those design support programs were artificial intelligence.

At Sargent & Lundy Engineers in the early 1970s, an understanding of computer programming and applications was required in order to work on advanced power engineering projects. During that period I was introduced to pin-registered overlay drafting by representatives of Cushing & Company. This use of and understanding of layers allowed for comprehensive description of three-dimensional spaces. At the same time, a working relationship with many related design disciplines provided an understanding of shared data and precision interference checking.

Once I had acquired this background as a production architect, the transition to coordinating the reprographics output from Ridgway's computer systems division (Entrec, now UDC) in Houston in the late 1970s was quite exhilarating and again most informative. What followed was numerous consulting service experiences concerning layering systems and drafting systems with members of the miniMAX Association and the International Reprographic Association. Assisting numerous architects, engineers, and design firms to obtain greater output from their manual and computerized drafting functions caused me to notice certain trends and similarities of need, which in turn led to this book.

From 1983 to 1985 my work as director of the Oliveri CADD Group in Hartford, Connecticut, reinforced concepts of useful output from both two-dimensional and three-dimensional CADD systems. We found that, in many companies, there was altogether too much emphasis on the impressiveness of CADD without any concept of how or where CADD systems should be applied. I hope that this book will be of assistance to those seeking to understand the practical aspects of applying CADD systems to design, drafting, and database management.

Technical acknowledgment goes also to Tandy Radio Shack and its licensed software programs SCRIPSIT and WORD, which allow me to generate word strings, and their necessary revisions, at a rate that far surpasses manual means. Using word processing also intimately reminds me of the lessons of softcopy document storage and retrieval—and the tragedy of unwanted electronic erasure. Special thanks is also extended to Georgia Kornbluth for editing this assemblage of nomenclature into a coherent whole.

CADD Systems Overview

Computer-aided design and drafting is what CADD is supposed to be. A CADD system is further considered to be an interactive computer-aided graphics system rather than merely an interactive computer-aided *electronic data processing* (EDP) system. Thus, CADD can handle the creation and manipulation of lines and curves as well as the usual alphanumeric characters. This ability to handle lines and curves is a prerequisite to proper design and drafting by computer.

As a tool in the design and drafting process, the computer should provide useful assistance in achieving the desired end results of both design and drafting. To accomplish the general task of design, a CADD system must be very flexible and must exhibit a wide range of image creation and display capabilities. To accomplish the drafting task, a CADD system must be very precise and provide consistent and workable output.

In applying and comparing CADD systems with the conventional manual design and drafting processes, CADD must be measured in similar terms of output. If a CADD system is introduced as an aid to and valuable assistant in the entire design process, it must show at least similar if not improved productivity over the manual methods that it is augmenting. Hence, a CADD system may be looked upon as a recently hired, or about to be hired, new member of the production staff.

Any new, lower-echelon staff member is often first used for filing functions and for simple, usually repetitious, drafting. Interestingly, performing these functions just happens to be a valuable asset of CADD systems. Also, office standards and procedures need to be learned and followed by the new recruit. The CADD system is introduced into the office environment as the newest, and presumably the most highly efficient, member.

How will the CADD system handle the same tasks as any other staff member? How will it adjust to and apply the established office standards of practice? These are the types of questions that are, or should be, normally considered when a CADD system is being put to use. Unfortunately, these questions have a personal connotation. Giving the CADD system humanlike qualities and attempting to put it to work as a rational, artificially intelligent thinking system are two of the first errors usually made in the transition to efficient computer-aided design and drafting.

As fully outlined in Chapter 3, any new CADD system must be considered as a computer-aided design (CAD) tool and separately as a computer-aided design and drafting (CADD) tool. The emphasis here should be on the word "tool." CADD is an *aid* to design and drafting, *not a replacement for the normal functions.* As such, CADD does not replace anyone, but rather, like an adjustable triangle, a calculator, or a track drafting machine, CADD should make the job of design and drafting easier and more productive.

1.1   From Drafting to CADD Layering

Conventional manual drafting is used to create a drawing or presentation form which is then used to communicate the design to the viewer. The viewer of the drawn form of the design can then determine whether the intent of the design has been communicated, can carry the design image to the next step in the review process, and, if required, can fabricate or construct the design; or can use the end product.

Basic drafting

Figure 1.1 lays out the sequence of events that occurs when the drafter receives input, creates a drawing, and subsequently has the drawn image reviewed before delivery as final output.

This sequence can be as simple and personal as providing command input to one's own hand to create, in hardcopy form, a design image that exists only as cerebral impulses. Or it may be taken as the form of events between the designer or engineer who gives input to the drafter, who delineates the hard-line form, submits the drawing back for review by the designer or engineer, incorporates all revisions, and then issues the drawing output as input to the next stage of design.

At this most basic level of drafting logic, the CADD system is applied as a simple electronic drafting aid and tool. The designer, engineer, architect or drafter as operator inputs commands to the CADD system which in turn displays the image for review.

A comparison of Figure 1.1 with Figure 1.2 shows that an extra step has been imposed upon the overall flow path in Figure 1.2. Whereas

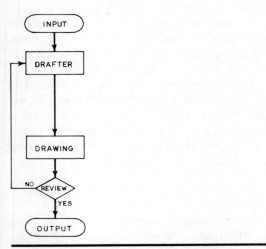

Figure 1.1 Conventional input and output.

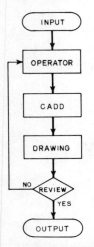

Figure 1.2 CADD input and output.

in the first instance the drafter is actively and manually creating the hardcopy drawing for subsequent review, Figure 1.2 includes the operator function, which directs the creation of the drawings on the CADD system before normally plotted or displayed review.

Note that for each figure, when the drawing review response is negative, the feedback flows correctly back to the drafter or operator rather than simply to the drawing. The reviewer's commentary may appear on the drawing as checker's notes, but the information is used by the drafter. Similarly, a review of drawings from a CADD system may elicit notations on the CADD drawing (plot), but the ultimate directive is to the operator rather than to the CADD unit.

Figure 1.3 provides the more generic logic path which holds the CADD system at the same status level as that of a drafting implement. Here the drafter who uses pens, pencils, stencils, and triangles is equivalent to the CADD operator who uses digitizer pucks, electromagnetic probes, keyboards, and menu pads. In today's offices the manual drafter and the CADD operator may be the same person, doing each job with the most suitable tools available. Thus a CADD system can be looked upon as a CADrafting tool, the best use of which must be learned and which need not be used at all times nor for all drafting efforts. This concept is further expanded in Chapter 7.

Repro-systems drafting

The intent of using support systems, rather than simply relying upon the manual ability to sketch, trace, and redraw valuable existing in-

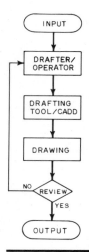

Figure 1.3 Combined input and output.

formation, is to save or reduce tedious redrafting man-hours so that that same valuable time can be utilized on more necessary or more rewarding tasks. The first step toward utilizing specialized systems as an aid to design and drafting is the use of reproduction methods to capture existing data.

Figure 1.4 follows the same logical flow path as Figure 1.1 but adds the parallel effort of reprographic restoration and duplication of existing drawing images. Rather than taking the time to redraw the pertinent elements of existing data fields, simple copies are made in the form of diazo, electrostatic and photographic (silver emulsion) erasable images. These copies then become the basic drawing backgrounds upon which the new design data is drawn.

The review process is the same here as in Figure 1.1 except for adding the normal extra step of reproducing the original as a checkprint upon which the reviewer or checker can add comments. This step helps to eliminate the risk of damaging the original drafted imagery. Feedback again is to the drafter, who incorporates the comments from the checkprint onto the original.

When CADD systems are applied to this scenario, the logic path changes to that shown in Figure 1.5. Similar in mode to Figure 1.2, the input control is still via the CADD operator, but the external, existing drawings are "restored" into the CADD system either by digitizing the pertinent points or by scanning the complete existing drawings and then editing the resultant captured database.

What was an external service function, reprographics restoration, in Figure 1.4 becomes an extra hardcopy handling effort for the CADD

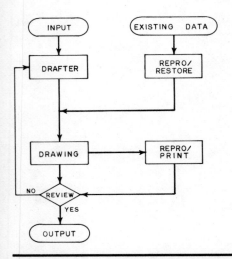

Figure 1.4 Conventional reprographic support.

operator. However, if the existing data is entered into the CADD system by digitizing, only the data which is required need be entered rather than worrying about a copy of a complete drawing which includes all the drafting foibles of the previous drafters.

Unfortunately, any scaling errors in the original may be captured in the electronic digitizing process, thus making further checking and editing necessary. Complete or partial existing-sheet electronic scanning also is subject to errors in scale caused by physical distortions and probably bad initial drafting. Scanning generally captures all data without differentiation and still requires extensive CADD operator editing to correctly separate specific lines and text into their respective disciplines, layers, and database attributes. (Refer to Section 5.1.)

Of special note in Figure 1.5 is the extra process function block labeled "Plot Hardcopy." For conventional manual drafting and repro-systems drafting, the drawing exists in real hardcopy form as a workable original which can be easily copied for multiple uses. The drawing on the CADD system exists as a regularized series of electromagnetic points, known as "bits" and "bytes," stored in electronic memory. To become a hardcopy for external multiple use, the CADD drawing must be plotted (in a variety of forms, as discussed in Chapter 5) onto a hardcopy format before normal reprographic printing.

However, a fully functioning CADD system does not require the hardcopy plot if the reviewer or checker can have access to the same CADD system database and call up the particular drawing, or a copy of the drawing, to a remote terminal for checking in an interactive graphic mode. This special attraction of the use of CADD is a part of

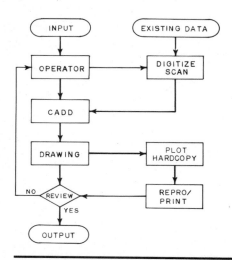

Figure 1.5 CADD with hardcopy handling.

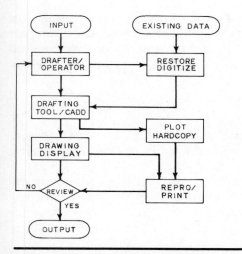

Figure 1.6 Combined hardcopy support.

the utopian "paperless office" concept which has yet to be fully implemented.

For fully functioning checking of CADD system drawings and for maximum productivity, multiple workstations or terminals in separate locations are required. Chapter 2 covers the sundry aspects of single or multiple CADD workstations and the networking of CADD systems.

Keeping to the theme of this book, Figure 1.6 incorporates the principal aspects of fundamental repro-systems drafting and CADD systems procedures into a coherent whole. Building on the logic of Figure 1.3, here the side themes of incorporating existing drawing images and of reproducing the initial output as checkprints are added to the main *input*-work-review-*output* flow path.

The new function of CADD hardcopy plotting, or redrawing of the database, is the only extra work element introduced by CADD. Digitizing of old data, although a "new" form, is really quite similar to the tracing of existing drawings. Hardcopy plotting, on the other hand, creates an "original" just for checking purposes; and then creates another "new original" for each additional issue.

This ability to quickly recreate hardcopy "originals" is a concept new to drafting. Under conventional manual methods, it would be a tremendous waste of time to throw away the current original drawing and totally redraw it just to make a simple revision. Yet this is precisely what occurs with normal CADD system plotting.

Whether the drawings are created by hand or via CADD, the initial output is reviewed either as display or as hardcopy, and resultant comments are returned to the drafter or operator. This do-loop function continues until all comments have been resolved. "Final" output for the figure must be considered as developing from the shortest, straight-line flow path only. The actual output from this figure then becomes input to the next applicable point in the design process (see Chapter 3). Few things are ever "final."

Layered systems

A more precise transition step from manual design and drafting techniques to CADD systems utilization is the use of pin-registered overlay drafting or pin graphics. The logic of layered systems drafting suggests that the common portion of a design image that is shared by several disciplines should be drawn on a separate sheet or layer which can then be precisely aligned (registered) with other physical sheets or layers. This sharing of registered layers is also one cornerstone of the CADD systems methodology.

Conventional pin graphics separates the drafter's input into selectively reusable layers (as shown in Figure 1.7). External data are included as photorestored and registered "existing" layers which are *drawn over* by the drafter. These several layers must be reprographically composited into a single complete sheet in order to make a coherent drawing for checkprinting for review purposes.

The checker or reviewer could also choose to study the actual individual layers which are held in alignment with the standard graphic arts 7-pin pinbar. Comments to a particular layer would be added directly to that layer, possibly with the use of a fade-out blue pencil.

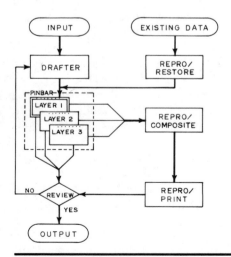

Figure 1.7 Pin graphic layers throughput.

Feedback to the drafter could be these notes on the specific layers, or could be revision notes on the composite prints which are then returned to the drafter.

Figure 1.8 portrays the same layered systems story. However, here the hero of the logic path is the operator's CADD system. Existing data is scanned or digitized into the database. Discrete and shared data elements are portrayed on separate, electromagnetically registered layers. The CADD layers are displayed as a composite image on the monitor screen, or cathode ray tube (CRT), for interactive checking and review.

Alternatively, these same or additional selected layers are composited in the plot file and then plotted onto hardcopy for repligraphics and checkprinting. An offline checker or reviewer could choose to study the individual layers, if plotted separately, or to work with the composite plot. Feedback to the CADD operator could be these notes on the composite images, or could be arranged as a separate "checking layer" within the system.

Figures 1.7 and 1.8 look surprisingly alike. They should, for their handling logic is the same. Pin graphics, or pin-registered overlay drafting, has been called "human-cadd"[A1] because each step in its utilization matches a similar step with CADD systems. CADD uses hardware, firmware, software, and operator's wetware to achieve the same net result as the manual system, pin graphics, with its use of a simple pinbar, registered polyester drafting film and also the drafter's wetware. *Wetware?* Without it—that gray matter between our ears—the other "wares" would not function very well.

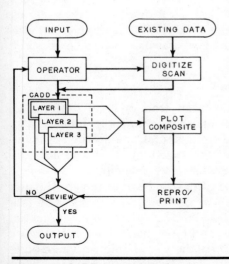

Figure 1.8 CADD layers throughput.

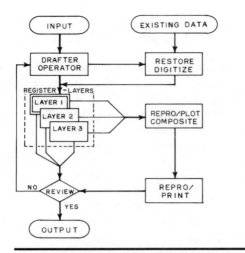

Figure 1.9. Layered systems drafting.

Figure 1.9 combines the processes of CADD and pin graphics to show the logic path of generic layered systems drafting. This figure incorporates all the logic steps from basic drafting through repro-systems drafting and pin graphics to CADD layering. The functions of manual drafting tools and the interactive graphics aid of CADD have become the dotted line surrounding the stacked and aligned layers.

Horizontal compositing to hardcopy plots or reprographic contact composites and photocomposites are the secondary or peripheral means of achieving a checkprint for reviewing purposes. The more direct composite form is the vertical flow path as a direct-displayed output of the layers as electromagnetic images on the CRT monitor. The more useful output may be the physical hardcopy, drawn or plotted "originals."

1.2   Data Logic and Graphics Logic

Bear in mind that, during the transition from manual drafting to computer-aided design and drafting, another, even more fundamental transition is occurring. Typically the architectural, engineering, or manufacturing design firm is also making the transition from a position of no general computer systems to the major use of computers.

Bypassing the traditional sand paintings and stone tablets, Figure 1.10 shows the transition from manual drafting of graphics and the handwriting or hand printing of text to the use of semiautomatic equipment such as drafting machines and typewriters. The logical next step, which is currently taking place, is the use of interactive graphic (and text) CADD units with computerized word processors and data manipulators.

Often, in the pressure to "automate" with CADD, a firm will attempt to overstep the very important issue of just using computers for the everyday tasks of word processing, accounting, filing, engineering calculations, and marketing. Before CADD, perhaps the only active computer systems in the office were hand-held and desktop calculators. The move up from these simple systems to micro- and mini-computer graphic and data processing systems is just as traumatic a change in office practice as would be the change from manual drafting to interactive computer-aided drafting.

Many lessons about the basic procedures and proper techniques for computer-aided work can be learned by implementing the use of a microcomputer for word processing and basic number-crunching spreadsheets. The cost of a simple word and data processing microcomputer hardware and software system is a fraction of the cost of a major CADD investment. Plus, some microsystems can be upgraded to handle rudimentary drafting graphics software or even interface with the mini- and mainframe systems for full CADD software use.

Data logic

For the purposes of this book and for a simplified understanding of computers in general and CADD specifically, the distinction must be made between *electronic data processing* (EDP) and *interactive graphics.*

Let data be considered as pertaining primarily to alphabetical and numerical characters, or alphanumerics. These alphanumeric character strings represent the notes, descriptions, and dimensions of a drawing. Let graphics be considered as pertaining to the lines and curves, the drawing image.

Standard data processing concerns the handling of alphanumeric character strings—word processing. Computer-aided design and drafting, on the other hand, requires the additional control of geometrical points in space. Add color to this mix, and the management requirements rise exponentially.

A computer can be considered as a very fast electromagnetic switching device with a very accurate memory of the relative and changeable ON/OFF positions of those switches. Of the two classes of computers, analog and digital, we will be dealing here with the digital type, in that the

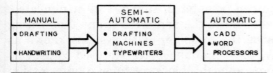

Figure 1.10 From manual to automatic.

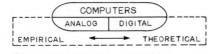

Figure 1.11 Digital versus analog data.

data- and graphics-handling conditions can be best controlled with YES/NO, ON/OFF information gates or switches.

As delineated in Figure 1.11, analog computers work primarily with empirically determined data which must be accumulated (summed) to provide investigation of and control over physical systems.[B1] Practical applications of analog computers include (1) flow monitoring in process piping, HVAC systems and (2) solving straightforward algebraic problems.

Digital computers handle information as a binary code. The term "binary" means that the data has two states, such as ON/OFF or YES/NO or GO/NOGO. Binary data is handled as *binary digits,* or *bits.* The binary digit, or bit, representation of a YES/NO condition or GATE/SWITCH is, for example, either a 1 (YES) or a 0 (NO). For a thorough discussion of general computer systems, refer to the *Encyclopedia of Computer Science and Engineering.*[B1]

Bit:	Binary digit	:	1 or 0 single unit
8 bits:	Byte	:	256 combinations
16 bits:	2 bytes	:	32,767 combinations
32 bits:	4 bytes	:	$2+x10^{10}$ combinations

Figure 1.12 A byte into bit ranges.

To handle alphanumeric data, these bits are arrayed in groups of 8 digits called "bytes." Digital computers can be classed by the number of bits they handle. As tabulated in Figure 1.12, an 8-bit, 1-byte digital machine can process and store units no greater than 256, whereas a 2-byte, 16-bit machine can handle a maximum numeric value of 32,767. Currently, most of the larger, faster digital computers are 32-bit, 4-byte digital computers which handle numbers and word groups in excess of 2 billion counters.[B2]

With sufficient combinations of ON/OFF, 1/0 bits, directions can be given and alphanumeric data can be entered, stored, and manipulated. These simple functions are adapted to the handwriting and typewriting functions to create and provide the computer-aided systems known as "word processing." Similarly, these bits and bytes are used to provide specifically addressable and programmable blocks or zones of information

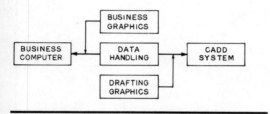

Figure 1.13 Graphics and the data process.

which can be spread out to simulate a ledger sheet for accounting purposes.

The typical CADD system computer is a collection of analog and digital microprocessors required to handle the various duties of electrical signal control and data processing.

Business graphics

Within the field of word processing and spreadsheet usage, business graphics provides the first realization of the "drafting" capabilities of the computer. Using "graphics" in the business sense means varying letter and number font sizes and types, geometrical charts, and graphical figures and of course controlling the color attributes.

Figure 1.13 shows that data handling is the core concept, with business graphics as a function of the general group of computers known as "business systems." On the engineering, architecture, and design side is the drafting graphics function which is the basis for CADD systems.

The first real change in normal semiautomatic and automatic output modes (as shown in Figure 1.10) occurs when business graphics is added to the standard computerized word processing systems. This can be a preliminary move toward electronic publishing.

All standard data-handling hardcopy output, being in common alphanumeric characters, is accomplished with daisy wheel, standard print wheel, or mechanical hammer font devices. Specialized font graphics, charts, and graphs with solid, filled-in areas require pen plotters and dot matrix printers to provide the necessary combinations of image points. As color is introduced, the necessary output device requirements increase dramatically. Refer to Chapter 5 for a complete discussion of hardcopy output.

Graphics logic

As the images of business graphics designs become more involved, the graphics sheets take on many of the aspects of engineering and architectural drawings. In reality the complicated business graphics become

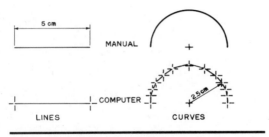

Figure 1.14 Manual versus computer imagery.

an assembly of discrete lines and curves as well as the original text (alphanumerics).

Figure 1.14 shows the logical differences between a 5-centimeter (1.995-inch) line drawn by hand and that same line segment drawn by the computer. The manually drawn line is created by starting the line at a measured point and then drafting (with graphite, plastic, ink, or tape) for a measured 5-centimeter (1.995-inch) distance. The drafting function is an implied recording function in that the line image has been physically transferred to the drafting medium for long-term retention.

To accomplish the same task in a digital computer manner, first the X and Y coordinates of the initial point must be defined by keyboard or cursor positioning. Then the terminating point's coordinates must be selected and designated. Finally, the vector or raster line segment must be generated between these two points. Concurrently, these coordinate points and line functions must be recorded in the computer system memory for later recall.

The line segment that is generated by computer between the two end points must be considered from two distinct output standpoints. First is the display mode to the CRT monitor. Take note that the display image of the line is a series of picture elements, *pixels,* which depict the line as a series of X and Y points. Second is the hardcopy output mode via the plotter. For further discussion of these points, refer to Chapters 3 and 5. An excellent demonstration of these images is found in Michael Schley's article, "CAD Buyer's Checklist."[A2]

Similarly, in Figure 1.14, a simple half-circle image with a 5-centimeter (1.995-inch) diameter can be drawn as a smooth curve with a compass set for a 2.5-centimeter (0.998-inch) radius commencing at a starting point and finishing, after a twirl of the fingers, at a predetermined end point.

The computer-generated semicircle again requires that each finite point on the curved line be determined, set, and recorded. The simple circular curve can be determined mathematically, and complex curves, or splines, can also be formulated. Typically, a microcomputer system works only as a digital system using binary, or two-function, elements. It can create straight-line segments, defined as distances between two points. Hence the half-circle curve line is actually a series of short straight-line segments which develop a circular form because they are very small facets. The higher the precision of the system and the higher the resolution of the display, the smoother and more uniform the curves and splines.

Whereas the hand-generated graphics image exists in a hardcopy form, the first CADD-generated image exists as an electronic projection on the CRT monitor. To obtain a comparable hardcopy form, the CADD system must be directed to plot (draft) a hardcopy. The vector-plotted hardcopy form of a simple half-circle image, 5 centimeters (1.995 inches in diameter) would show a smooth-curve circle because of the curve-forming algorithms in the plotter firmware. A raster-plotted hardcopy image of the half-circle form may appear to be similar to the monitor display image, a series of short facets, depending upon the available resolution.

Figure 1.15 compares the relative images of a manually generated 45° line and a semicircle line with those of vector and raster plots and that of the CRT monitor display image. Vector-controlled pen plots provide the closest similarity to conventional manual drafting.

Raster plots which represent images with discrete dots can show quite smooth lines and curves if the dot resolution is greater than 200 dots per inch (dpi). Current state of the art puts electrostatic images in the 400-dpi range. Usually the lowest resolution is that of the CADD terminal or CRT, even at 1024×1024 pixels; hence this figure shows the greatest number of "jaggies" (forced offsets due to pixel count).

1.3   Minimum Software and Hardware Packages

To allow a designer using CADD to closely emulate the work of a human designer, several minimum software, firmware, and hardware

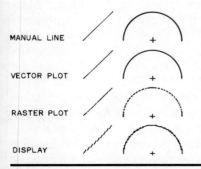

MANUAL LINE

VECTOR PLOT

RASTER PLOT

DISPLAY

Figure 1.15 Vector versus raster images.

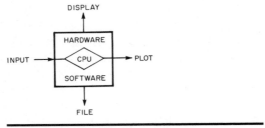

Figure 1.16 Hardware-software output forms.

packages are required to perform adequate design functions. Similarly, CADD the drafter must have certain basic drafting functions (tools) in order to act in support of the human drafter.

For a CADD system to be productive, input via the hardware to the software which is then to be manipulated by the *central processing unit* (CPU) must be displayed for interactive viewing, must be filed, must be recallable from file for reuse, and usually requires a hardcopy plot output for offline functions.

Each of these functions—input, display, file, and plot—requires interchange between hardware and software to be smooth and consistent. While the software is very important, the designer is actually always in touch with the hardware. This combination of touching the hardware and using the software varies depending upon whether the designing or drafting is being done with the computer's assistance.

To draft by design

Designing with CADD assistance, which is primarily software-dependent, requires an attention to machine functions that may prove to be a hindrance to the designer's normal freedom of movement and use of intellect—qualities that are a hallmark of design.

Sketching and other free-flowing, paintbrush-style or rendered-line moves are not easily accomplished with micro-CADD systems nor even with some mini- and mainframe systems. (However, the simple Macintosh system seems to do this quite well!) Alternative design proposal images, schemes, and layouts, on the other hand, are very well suited to the CADD environment. Once the images are in place within the database, multiple copies, each with minor or major modifications, are readily available and easily displayed.

Drafting with CADD assistance becomes an enjoyable occupation as compared with the tedium of conventional efforts. CADD provides a qualified designer or drafter with the tools necessary to work at a pace which is much closer to the human thinking process. In the drafting function, the use of CADD is quite hardware-dependent. Input functions require various interconnected devices, visual display is required to monitor input and review, and hardcopy output is almost entirely a hardware function.

Figure 1.17 lays out the logic flow from input to design for the three-dimensional world to hardcopy output in a two-dimensional format. The drafting function directly interfaces with system hardware while being supported by software. Design efforts rely upon the software with its display and manipulation of images via the hardware.

Minimum software

Software is the first CADD support system to be considered. Without the proper programming and system functions, the use of computers as an aid to design and drafting would not be viable. Start first with simple design efforts based upon redefining the use of simple two-dimensional drafted images, and only then move on to three dimensions. The advantages of three dimensions allow designing and drafting with wire frames, surface definitions, and solids modeling. But three-dimensional work becomes productive only after the operator develops a full understanding of the capability of the particular CADD system and a thorough conception of solid geometry.

Keeping in mind that CADD is to be used as an increased output tool, computer-assisted drafting functionally begins before use of computer-assisted spatial design or three-dimensional graphics. The groups of lines and text to be considered for design purposes must first be entered in two dimensions or generated by the computer's drafting graphics with the necessary X and Y (and Z) coordinates. Then the available software should perform the design tasks required.

Figure 1.18 provides a simple checklist for creating graphic lines and handling text in a two-dimensional environment. All these actions are normally available for micro-CADD systems. Take special note of the

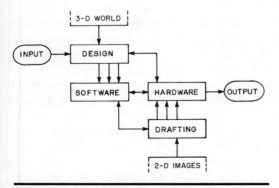

Figure 1.17 Software-hardware flow.

[ ] Get drawing or sheet.	[ ] Save drawing or sheet.
[ ] Select item or point.	[ ] Move item or point.
[ ] Set scale.	[ ] Set layer.
[ ] COPY.	[ ] DELETE.
[ ] OOPS! (escape or cancel).	[ ] Set color.
[ ] Rotate.	[ ] Mirror.
[ ] Set protractor: distance angle.	[ ] Define window.
[ ] Define group of elements.	[ ] Pan and zoom.
[ ] Define circles and arcs.	[ ] Join or split elements.
[ ] Define smooth curve splines.	[ ] Fillet radius.
[ ] Create plot file.	[ ] Merge drawing files.

Figure 1.18 Minimum two-dimensional line and text manipulations.

OOPS! command. This is an "escape" or "cancel" command that negates *only the immediately previous command* which may have been an error. This software effort requires a concurrent commands field, the last 5 or more commands, to restore the workstation to the previous data-display position.

Two-dimensional versus three-dimensional imaging

Three-dimensional imaging in CADD systems allows for excellent graphic modeling of the part, assembly, or complete facility. This can assist in design analysis, clearance verification, and presentations to clients. However, the subsequent communication of a design with the visual flat-plane displays and plotted hardcopy documents is primarily a two-dimensional representation of that three-dimensional data.

True three-dimensional hardcopy is sculpture—a freezing of the rhythm of design into the dynamic interplay of static elements. In this sense, CADD output via numeric control directly to milling machines and other fabrication efforts, including robotics, comes closest to three-dimensional drafting.

Full design is, however, a three-dimensional effort with control over spatial relationships. Tolerance comparisons of designs, facilities, full machine assembiles, and subassembly parts also require conceptualization in three dimensions. Thus, to best accomplish a minimum design task, both two- and three-dimensional software are necessary.

A CADD system should allow multilayer, multicolor three-dimensional imaging for design work, then should provide a direct transition to two-dimensional representation for the high-volume needs of each specific discipline's monochrome hardcopy communication. Imaging may start in two dimensions, proceed to three-dimensional manipulation, and return to two dimensions for hardcopy plotting.

If only computer-assisted drafting work is required, it can be easily accomplished with simple, two-dimensional, monochrome CADD systems. The extra expense of three dimensions can be held off until the CADD system is truly paying for itself.

Additional software

If not included in the basic two-dimensional CADD system software, *automatic dimensioning* is the first upgraded software package that should be acquired. Since the X and Y coordinates of every line and curve reference point are already a part of the database, capturing and displaying relative point distances is comparatively easy.

If several portions of a design or detail can be reused with the same general shape but with slightly different dimensions, *variational geometry* software may be a beneficial add-on. This software program uses assigned variables for each of the principal dimensions of the selected shape. A general command can be used to recall the shape's image, including the new specific dimensions which would then be ready for alternate uses.

It is beyond the scope of this book to dwell in depth on the many applications for *relational database management*.[B3] This software subject is covered by the numerous texts listed in the reference sections at the end of the book and is also discussed in Chapter 4. Designs and especially drawings created with *intelligent lines* and *intelligent text* will communicate far better than the traditional, manually created drawings or even simple CADrafting-generated drawings. All of CADD is moving in the direction of thorough relational database management of images. Start early to understand these data-handling procedures, and actively incorporate as many of them as possible.

To truly integrate the visual and esthetic aspects of design with the mechanical and structural analysis of the physical elements of the design, *finite element analysis* (FEA) is a software system that can be used to help define the precise contours of a shape as well as to determine physical stresses.[A3] Working essentially in a three-dimensional environment, FEA software can be used to isolate specific portions of a design and to accumulate forces over a large area.

Firmware

Normally the available software programs are loaded into the computer system via floppy disks or tape reels. The actual software program instructions are magnetically encoded onto the disks or tapes. The disks or tapes act as a transport mechanism for storage and retrieval of the sequenced data. As such, they are remote or separate from the computer system.

When these software programs are physically incorporated into the computer system, by encoding the programs onto *read-only memory* (ROM), they are given the additional designation *firmware*. Most often found as word processing, spreadsheet, and Basic programs, this resident firmware is integrated within the central processing unit (CPU) or is provided as *add-on* boards or chips. Current technology is providing these ROM chips with programmable features which allow practical modifications, such as erasability and reprogrammability, to these otherwise fixed assets.

Hardware display functions—such as cursor image control, color imaging support, displayed image memory, and display manipulation—are typically handled by the firmware at the terminal. These functions may differ from, enhance, or detract from the related software-driven imaging functions. Determine the mix and limits of the firmware display functions of your CADD system.

Minimum hardware

After first selecting the desired software, then and only then should you choose the hardware that will support the software requirements. Purchasing the hardware first may cause unnecessary setup time and even require purchase of extra software interface programs in order to properly operate the desired design and drafting system. Consider the minimum hardware required for computer-assisted design and drafting.

The heart of the system is the central processing unit where the commands are translated into machine code by the controller software. To this is fed the software and the design and drafting input. As shown in Figure 1.19, the CPU has many service peripherals in order to provide means for data input and to provide output such as a display of what is happening with the software and the database.

To many people in the computer industry, the term "output" often means only "output to display (monitor)." This "display output" is relevant for interactive graphics, but "hardcopy output" may be as relevant if not more relevant for designers and drafters.[S1] Thus, one of the important peripherals diagrammed in Figure 1.19 is the hardcopy

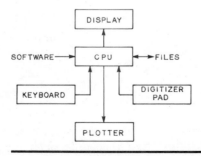

Figure 1.19 Functions to and from the CPU.

device, the printer or plotter. Refer to Chapters 3 and 5 for more information on these subjects.

Figure 1.20 shows a simple but typical minicomputer interactive system block diagram capable of handling the basic input-work-output equation required for proper application of CADD interactive graphics. While input to a conventional drawing may be via pen or pencil, input to the CADD system can be via an electronic probe pen from the menu tablet or digitizer board or directly via the keyboard.

In addition, input can be from the light-source probe pen or even a finger via an interactive CRT screen. Input to the CADD memory or database is further available from various disk, tape, and cassette devices by hardwire or telephone modem. This external memory interface provides a depth of data and direct calculation and analysis that is unknown to conventional drawing.[S1, S2]

Figures 1.21 and 1.22 give generic views of what the micro-CADD operator would find on his or her desk in lieu of the traditional drafting machine and adjustable triangle. The menu pad with probe pen, which allows preset commands to be quickly selected, is a digital input device that can also be used for digitizing existing data. Also in Figure 1.21 is a joystick for cursor control and the standard keyboard for data and command entry. Output is to the CRT display.

The slight modifications in Figure 1.22 include a larger digitizing pad with cursor control and a data input device known as a "mouse" or "puck." While the omnipresent CRT display and keyboard are included, note that the keyboard could include thumb wheels or a roller ("track") ball for cursor control. Preset menu commands would in this case normally be found displayed by the software on the CRT screen with selection by cursor control. Alternatively, common commands could be maintained with function keys on the keyboard.

Hardcopy output

Output from the CADD system, as shown in Figure 1.20, can be as softcopy electromagnetically delivered to the disks, tapes, and cassettes or as hardcopy delivered via plotters, computer output to microfilm (COM) devices, and printers. It should be pointed out that the output mode noted as "thermographic 'quick look'" (Figure 1.20) is the same as or is similar to the "hardcopy readout" below the interactive CRT on the input side of the diagram.[S1]

The hardcopy output from the printer or plotter modes returns the data from the CADD system to a state similar to that of the "original" drawing in conventional drafting. At this point the CADD hardcopy, like the product of conventional drafting, can be visually inspected in its entirety or further reproduced as required.

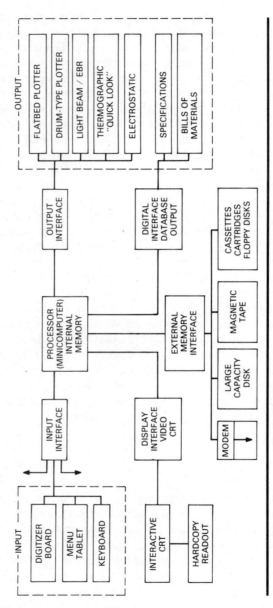

Figure 1.20 Interactive system block diagram.

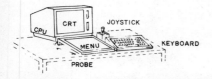

Figure 1.21 Simple hardware arrangement.

Figure 1.22 Hardware with digitizer.

On the hardcopy output side of Figure 1.20, note that the devices are controlled as two distinct and separate functions. At the top of the diagram are the graphic output devices for lines and curves as well as text. Within the same dotted outline but initiated from a digital interface is the output to alphanumeric imaging devices such as daisy wheel and dot matrix printers. These forms primarily handle text output only.

Monochrome or color display

The majority of design documents are communicated to the fabricator or constructor, client or consumer, and code authorities by means of monochromatic imaging: blue lines on a white field, black lines on a white field, or white or clear lines on a black or opaque field. Color may communicate multiple concepts better than monochrome, but the cost is higher and the user's learning curve is longer and steeper.

Take a close look at Section 4.4 for the discussions of how color communicates. Because the CADD system both handles and presents such a vast amount of precise data, a color display monitor should be the basic choice for a CADD workstation. "Hundreds" and "millions" of color combinations are not required for typical CADD work. Rather, a minimum of seven or eight primary colors is all that is necessary, *provided that those colors can be assigned to different line types, text types, layers, and logical pens.* Also, the ability of the CADD workstation display terminal to provide antialiasing will functionally increase the apparent color resolution and smooth out adjacent color fields.[A4, A5, A6]

However, much of the hardcopy output from CADD is monochrome, and the color display images must be coordinated with the standard plotter output.[A7] Section 5.1 provides examples of how black-and-white output can be strictly matched to its color display.

Chapter

2

CADD Acquisition Management

Adding the CADD system to a design and drafting office is much like acquiring a new staff member. Not only must the new member have good credentials and be able to do the required job, but she or he or it (in this case) must be cost-justifiable.

The first thoughts usually relate to how much the new acquisition is going to cost. Then the emphasis changes to the more pertinent discussion of how the new acquisition is to be used. Perhaps, like choosing the proper software before paying for the necessary hardware, we can reorient this old line of reasoning toward reviewing function and use as the justification for investment. To consider the end result of CADD first, before making a purchase or other acquisition, allows not only cost justification but also best-use application.

2.1 Project Cost Controls

Starter sets for computer-aided drafting systems can be found from $5000 to $12,000 including a small-format printer and plotter. Low-cost systems that can perform drafting and design tasks, a truer CADD system, begin around $11,000 and range up through $30,000. For real sophistication in functions, color, and database management, budget figures can range from $25,000 through $90,000. These numbers are for the first complete workstation. Additional workstations with equal CADD capabilities may cost from 50 to 100 percent as much as the first unit.

With basic CADD systems software and hardware costs in the range from $5000 to $90,000, it is easy to see why CADD system acquisition can be closely equated with the decision to take on a new employee. Also, as with an employee, the direct wages paid to the employee or the monthly payments to the bank for the CADD system do not include the extra payments for insurance, taxes, and maintenance expenses. In addition, with the CADD system, personnel training expenses and lost time and revenue from normal production must be considered.

Thus, it may be wise to establish a method for keeping track of all expenses for the anticipated CADD system before acquisition. If this analysis is set up without regard to any actual figures, it can be applied not only to further human or equipment acquisitions but also to other aspects of the design and drafting profession. This methodology is manifested in the concept of a *cost center*.

INITIAL SOFTWARE	CPU HARDWARE
Purchase	Purchase
Finance	Finance
Insurance	Insurance
Maintenance	Maintenance
ADDITIONAL SOFTWARE	TERMINAL HARDWARE
Purchase	Purchase
Finance	Finance
Insurance	Insurance
Maintenance	Maintenance
MEMORY SYSTEMS	PLOTTER HARDWARE
Purchase	Purchase
Finance	Finance
Insurance	Insurance
Maintenance	Maintenance
Supplies	Supplies
PERSONNEL	PHYSICAL PLANT
Wages plus	Space rental
Training	Utilities
Supplies	Insurance
Lost productivity	Maintenance

Figure 2.1 CADD cost-center checklist.

Use Figure 2.1 as a guide for establishing your own cost center for a CADD system. Each line item should be given an entry, even if it is $0.00. Further differentiation of line items with pertinent subsets is fine, provided that their entries are reflected in the monthly, average, and annualized totals.

To help adjust to the use of computers and to ease the study of alternate systems, with their differing cost figures and subsequent impacts on the bottom-line return on investment (ROI), *set up the cost-center analysis on a computerized spreadsheet*. Do this for each workstation and peripheral to be considered. Allow provision for monthly data input and future incremental add-ons, and sum the totals in such a way that their data results can be interchanged with other spreadsheets that will help determine overall use rates and chargeable fee structures (if applicable).

Compare with current effort

To properly compare the CADD cost center, including its net costs and return on investment (ROI), with current production efforts, a project-by-project application review must be made. For most design and drafting firms this review can be quickly determined by choosing the project that will be using the CADD system. Then determine what portion of the project's designs and drawings will utilize CADD and what workforce would be required for both the manual and CADD portions.

Project name and number being considered for CADD?
   Project name: _____
   Project number: _____

Total number of project design drawings?   _____

Total number of project production drawings?   _____

Average hourly cost* to produce design drawings? $ _____

Average hourly cost* for production drawings? $ _____

Duration of project design portion, in months?   _____

Duration of project production phase, in months?   _____

Expected percentage of design drawings using CADD?   _____%

Expected percentage of production drawings using CADD?   _____%

   * For hourly cost, use the average technical hourly rate, the average multiple of direct expense figure, or both.

Figure 2.2 Basic comparison data to be determined before acquiring CADD.

Figure 2.2 provides a very short series of primary questions which must be answered in order to determine the applicability of CADD and the basis on which to allow its comparison with current efforts. The first question, "Project name and number being considered for CADD?", is often the first major stumbling block. As discussed in Chapter 3, the application of a CADD system requires a definitive "someplace" for it to be applied. This specific project, or project portion, will then allow for a more precise comparison of hours and costs.

On a separate piece of paper, follow Figure 2.2 by providing answers for your office and for a recently completed or about-to-be-started project. *Do not continue further in this book until you have answered these questions.* Approximate numbers and quantities are fine.

If you do not have a handle on these basic facts about your project, proper acquisition and application of a CADD system will probably elude your office. Plus, any purchase or other commitment will probably also fail to provide an adequate ROI.

Expanded comparison checklist

To analyze the ROI with CADD, it may be prudent to start with an even more in-depth analysis of current conventional drafting output so that a thorough standard for comparison can be established. Figure 2.3 provides a sequence of line items for reviewing conventional work with an eye toward applying CADD systems. A value can and should be found for each of these line items; if $0.00 is appropriate, use it.

As discussed in Chapter 1, a CADD system can be considered as just another systems drafting method which should save drafting time, increase productivity, and provide better document communications. Hence, not just conventional manual drafting but also the various reprographic drafting systems must be considered as the alternative to, or partner with, CADD. Bear in mind that most design and drafting firms are already using these advanced image-communication methods.

The time and cost studies required to track drafting production work-hours for conventional methods versus special reprographic systems and overlay methods before CADD may require an additional full-time clerk or secretary to keep a close record of the project teams and values involved. The extra work-hours of this employee should be included as additional drawing-handling time in Figure 2.3 under item 3b.[S1, S2]

This productivity review should normally be conducted or completed as one project is finished and before the next is started. In any case, an understanding of these factors must be available before you try to justify or implement a CADD system. Experience has shown that an average office might expect that nonconventional, but still hand-drawn, reprographic systems should average 36 percent more productive in their

1. Time and cost basis for current standard drawings output
   a. Number of drawings required to produce project
   b. Design and engineering hours required
   c. Drafting and checking hours required
   d. Checking and revision hours used

2. Time and cost comparison to draft at a common scale
   a. Additional drawings required
   b. Weighted drafting time due to more or less data per sheet
   c. Additional hours required to handle new drawings
   d. Drafting and checking hours saved at common scale
   e. Checking and revision hours saved at common scale

3. Time and cost comparison to draft using registered overlays
   a. Additional drafting film layers required
   b. Additional hours required to handle drawings
   c. Special planning-meeting time required
   d. Time required to correct layering mistakes
   e. Drafting and checking hours saved on common layers
   f. Checking and revision hours saved by disciplines

4. Time and cost comparison for project reproduction
   a. Current standard reproduction costs plus average costs
   b. Special handling, codifying, and auditing of drawings
   c. Specialized ordering requirements time
   d. Special reproduction and supplies costs
   e. Reproduction turnaround time impact

Figure 2.3 Tracking drafting production work-hours.

portion of contract documents and production drawings and 15 percent more productive overall.

Figure 2.4 takes the suggested format for conventional design and production drawings shown in Figure 2.3 and reviews the similar functions as augmented with a CADD system. The secondary sections dealing with special reprographics or pin graphics layering can be deleted or enhanced to suit project conditions and any mix of CADD with non-CADD systems. These concepts are covered in Chapter 7. It is recommended that the section on reproduction costs be included in each case since the CADD system's plotted hardcopy handling will have a serious impact on these figures.

These lists are expressed in general terms to allow for specific company formats. The order of data entry will probably need to be revised to suit individual office financial practices. Remember to use an electronic spreadsheet to facilitate this work.

The CADD workstation should be treated as if it were a drafting station with a very fast drafter, so that its output can be measured relative to that of a typical workstation. It may be found that although data input to a CADD system rapidly approaches normal drafting, it still lags because of deficiencies in the operator's training or experience on the equipment. Schematic and preliminary design studies and construction documents modifications are handled so much more rapidly with CADD that comparisons of time and cost with conventional methods may seem to lose meaning.[S1, S2]

Return on investment

Overall average return on investment in CADD should be in the range of 2:1 to 3:1. However, initial drafting-input speed on the CRT may be only 1:1 at best. The time required to produce a project should drop by an order of magnitude sufficient to easily justify a $55 to $85 per hour per workstation cost for a major CADD system which would include two- and three-dimensional capability, plus modeling and a database management system (DBMS).

Just who are the practitioners who would witness and participate in this ROI? To correlate the use of CADD directly with a project, it may be wise to consider not just which phase but also which person or function is affected. Figure 2.5 tabulates the general personnel func-

---

1. Time and cost basis for drawings output via CADD systems
   a. Number of CADD drawings required to produce project
   b. Special planning-meeting time required
   c. Computer-aided design hours required
   d. Computer-aided engineering hours (plus CAT) required
   e. CADD drafting, checking, and revision hours required
   f. CAD/CAM production throughput hours used

2. Time and cost comparison for drafting non-CADD project documents
   a. Additional conventional hand-drawn drawings required
   b. Weighted drafting time caused by more or less data per sheet
   c. Additional hours required to handle intermix of CADD and non-CADD drawings

3. Time and cost comparison for drafting with registered overlays
   a. Additional hand-drafting film layers required
   b. Additional CADD-generated film layers required
   c. Additional hours required to handle drawings
   d. Special planning-meeting time required
   e. Time required to correct layering mistakes
   f. Drafting and checking hours saved on common layers
   g. Checking and revision hours saved by disciplines

4. Time and cost comparison for project reproduction
   a. Current standard reproduction costs, plus average costs
   b. Special handling, codifying, and auditing of drawings
   c. Specialized ordering requirements time
   d. Special repligraphics interface costs and savings
   e. Special reproduction and supplies costs
   f. Reproduction turnaround time impact

Figure 2.4 Tracking manual and CADD production costs.

Personnel duties or function	Number per project	Average hourly cost	Average hours per drawing	CADD output factor*
Project manager	_____	$_____	_____	1.10
Project engineer	_____	$_____	_____	1.15
Project architect	_____	$_____	_____	1.15
Engineers	_____	$_____	_____	1.35
Architects	_____	$_____	_____	1.35
Designers	_____	$_____	_____	1.50
Checkers	_____	$_____	_____	1.90
Drafters	_____	$_____	_____	1.90
Clerks and staff	_____	$_____	_____	0.95

* Anticipated productivity increase or decrease factor.

Figure 2.5 Personnel functions, costs, and productivity.

tions that would interface with CADD but are here analyzed relative to their numbers, costs, and estimated hours spent per average drawing.

Each function, from project manager to clerk, would be affected by the use of CADD on a project. Using the chart of Figure 2.5 as a reference, make a list of the average direct-expense costs of your personnel. If your office functions with more categories per project, add them to the list. If one or more of those listed do not apply, leave them off. If a function occurs on one project but not another, leave it on the list but fill in the data as "0.00" (when it does not apply).

Determine the average number of hours each person would spend on the average drawing. Correlate this item with the data from Figure 2.2 to verify average hours budgeted for each drawing. (Further correlation could be extended to average hours per drawing per project phase, as shown in Figure 3.3.)

The right-hand column of Figure 2.5 includes an approximation of the current impact that CADD would have on each of these project functions. Overall project productivity with CADD may be hard to determine realistically. A possibly closer figure can be found for the individual activities. The numbers shown would certainly vary depending on the relative levels of CADD use per each function.

The highest probable productivity increase, 1.90, is accorded to the checking and drafting functions because of CADD system efficiencies and early payback results in these areas. The designer functions receive the next best figure, 1.50, for their anticipated multiple "what-if" actions, three-dimensional massing and color-imaging possibilities.

The remaining output productivity factors are established according to the person's proximity to the use of the CADD system. Better data communication may only slightly impact upon the project manager, who would be relying upon staff to do the actual work. Project engineers and architects could be impacted by database management system reports that may be associated with the CADD software. They might even be found taking a direct hand, or probe, at the workstation.

It is interesting to note that the clerk and staff functions may find that their normal productivity is *decreased* by CADD because of the increased number and type of drawings being created. In addition, they may be called upon to play nursemaid to the plotting function.

CADD applications benefits

Secondary benefits may be found in CADD's ability to produce multiple what-if drawings based on the initial design scheme. These "benefits" could become detriments if those additional drawings were not taken into account during estimates of drawings per project, work-hours per drawing, and project reproduction cost figures.

For example, creating a new drawing type for each aspect of a complex facility requiring numerous pieces of machinery may greatly facilitate construction coordination. To do this by manual drafting methods, with the necessary checking procedures, may require more work-hours than allowed by budget. However, by recalling and replicating to a new CADD sheet the shared plan images or layers as base reference, the redrafting and rechecking is substantially reduced.

Some multiple drawing types, which share the same background images, would be found in the following example:

- Facility plan and physical arrangement drawing
- Structural plan
- Grounding plan with specific ground-lugs positioning
- Buried piping plan
- Piping and electrical penetrations plan
- Electrical equipment plan
- Electrical power plan
- Electrical lighting plan
- Mechanical piping (large diameter) systems plan
- Mechanical piping (small diameter) systems plan
- Instrumentation sheet

With just the grounding layout and annotation as the foreground layer (possibly in different color?) over the equipment layout, a very much clearer set of drawings would be available for the electrical subcontractors. By adding these extra drawings, even greater productivity can be achieved, but extra care is required to keep track of the total work-hours expended.

When the "new" drawings are de-spooled to the plotter and the backup time-cost report shows minimal design and drafting (plotting) time used, even the most skeptical project directors should be amazed at the turnaround time. Comparison with conventional drawings shows that such additional, specialized CADD drawings could not be produced under the time schedule and budget constraints of conventional production methods without resorting to the extensive use of pin-registered layered drawings.

One spin-off from the initiation of CADD with a full-functioning DBMS that has had a positive impact on the project scheduling is precisely this time-on-system, drawings-per-project time study considered in Figure 2.4. When set up as a hidden tracking function in the DBMS, this cost-control analysis can print out the actual time used for each step in design and production without additional personnel.

What may have started as a review of conventional production methods can be updated to an online computerized review of current productivity—but by machine. Thus the "extra" clerk or secretary becomes available for additional and equally productive endeavors.

2.2 Project Application Checklists

To manage the most productive acquisition of a CADD system, some preliminary planning must be accomplished. This planning should take the form of a thorough consideration of how a computer-aided design and drafting system would be applied at each of the major stages in a project. Indeed, this applications review should begin well before system acquisition.

The main sequence—design, draft, estimate, fabricate—shown in Figure 2.6 can be effected first by the acquisition and then by the first application of the CADD system. Should it be used for designing or drafting? Should the parallel issues of materials specifications and

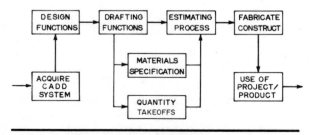

Figure 2.6 Functional stages in CADD usage.

quantity takeoffs be supported by a CADD system's database management functions for a more precise estimation process? Using CADD, the project or product can be constructed or fabricated quicker, less expensively, and with better quality.

Obtaining CADD

Use the Figure 2.7 checklist as a "Have you done this?" review before you begin actually to obtain a CADD system. Treat each item as a standard YES/NO gate in order to assure that all aspects have been considered. If the response is YES, pursue all ramifications until the file is exhausted. If the honest response is NO, stop at that point and reach a decision or complete the requested or implied task.

Applying CADD

Anticipating the methods that will be covered in Chapter 3, use the checklist shown in Figure 2.8 to help analyze precisely how and at what point in each particular project the CADD system will be applied. By breaking down the often rather intimidating complete picture of how CADD is to be applied into its finite elements, a very clear understanding of proper systems application can be achieved.

Again apply the YES/NO decision gate concept to each item in the following (short-form) list. A YES decision means that the CADD

Have you:	Yes	No
▪ Established a committee and procedures for CADD acquisition?	____	____
▪ Set and followed a selection criteria for system software?	____	____
▪ Set and followed a selection criteria for system hardware?	____	____
▪ Reviewed all similar CADD systems?	____	____
▪ Qualified all selected CADD vendors?	____	____
▪ Determined viability of nearby CADD service bureaus?	____	____
▪ Created a CADD system cost center?	____	____
▪ Established a plan for orderly transition to CADD?	____	____
▪ Established a proper CADD operator training program?	____	____
▪ Set a CADD system installation schedule?	____	____
▪ Set a CADD implementation schedule?	____	____
▪ Set a schedule for which projects are to use CADD, and when?	____	____

Figure 2.7 Action list to be performed before obtaining CADD.

Will the CADD system be used:	Yes	No
▪ For design analysis?	____	____
▪ For design presentation?	____	____
▪ For production drafting?	____	____
▪ For all project phases?	____	____
▪ For construction or fabrication monitoring?	____	____
▪ For construction or fabrication management?	____	____
▪ For constructor or fabricator needs?	____	____
▪ For specific client needs?	____	____
▪ For bill-of-materials and quantity takeoffs?	____	____
▪ For space planning?	____	____
▪ For facilities management?	____	____
▪ With graphics and data interface?	____	____
▪ With multiple locations?	____	____

Figure 2.8   Action list for applying CADD.

system must have the software and hardware capabilities to solve the problems inherent in that phase of design or drafting. A NO decision only sets that portion aside for the time being; perhaps that particular point will become a future use requirement.

Design applications

If the anticipated, or already acquired, CADD system is to be used for the design portions of a project, then perhaps an itemization of the several design functions will help to point out just where CADD will be applied. The design functions listed in Figure 2.9 cover a very wide range that would be applicable to architects, manufacturing designers, and engineers. Choose the aspects that relate to your office practices and your comprehensive service capabilities.

A YES decision on an item means that the CADD system must have the alphanumeric and graphic capabilities to solve the problems inherent in that design phase. A NO decision switches the action to another function and probably deletes those particular design functions from the "necessary" list for your system.

Drafting applications

Part of the physical act, though not necessarily the mental act, of designing entails the use of drafting methods and drafting tools. To design with a CADD system requires the intimate use of electronic drafting methods. Hence it must be noted that the list of design functions shown in Figure 2.9 should be traversed again, this second time with the specific drafting aspects foremost in mind.

Figure 2.10 provides categories for physical arrangement of drawings and plans. In this area are those sheets which require the generation of new work and revisions to existing images. For the most part, this drafting function is associated with hardcopy and other forms of existing databases.

Will the CADD systems be a drafting system (YES) or a design system (NO—not this kind of drafting tool)? Here the YES/NO gate provides useful directions and answers that anticipate real, usable output from the CADD system.

Real-time usage

If the foregoing checklists and qualification gates seem to apply to generalized situations, then consider these hands-on and real-time (or current) conditions. The following situations occur in offices which presently have CADD systems. Knowing what these concerns are before acquisition of a CADD system may help to avoid some simple mistakes.

- Does the hardware function in an ergonomic manner with the system operator? Easy and convenient keyboard layout, good resolution and

Are design functions required for:	Yes	No
• Feasibility studies?	——	——
• Financial analysis?	——	——
• Location analysis?	——	——
• Operations programming?	——	——
• Facilities programming?	——	——
• Design presentations?	——	——
• Schematic programming?	——	——
• Concept development?	——	——
• Engineering schematics?	——	——
• Piping and instrument diagrams?	——	——
• Single-line flow diagrams?	——	——
• Complete process diagrams?	——	——
• General arrangements?	——	——
• Mechanical and electrical loadings?	——	——
• Civil and structural loadings?	——	——
• Adjacency requirements?	——	——

Figure 2.9 Action list for designing with CADD.

Will the CADD system be used to produce:	Yes	No
• Concept and programming layouts?	____	____
• Preliminary plans and details?	____	____
• Presentation drawings?	____	____
• Design development drawings?	____	____
• Detail design and verification?	____	____
• Contract documents?	____	____
• Production documents?	____	____
• Plan and profile sheets?	____	____
• Facility elevations?	____	____
• Section and detail sheets?	____	____
• Finish and fixture schedules?	____	____
• System isometrics?	____	____
• Fabrication drawings?	____	____

Figure 2.10 Action list for drafting with CADD.

clear monitor-CRT, accessible yet quiet CPU and floppy disk or tape drives, and sufficiently large and accurate digitizer surface and input devices (probe pen or mouse) are all aspects of a well-functioning system.

- Does the software function with the expected ease and accurate response? Menu commands should be coherent and readily modifiable, control of graphics and text must be precise and responsive, and system defaults and memory handling must act to maintain data integrity protection.

- If database management is a basic aspect of the CADD system, do all graphic lines and curves and all text types and groups have assignable attributes which help to make a truly intelligent drawing? Are the drawing and sheet images composed of layers, colors, logical pens, and embedded instructions a representation of the database or merely an electronic drafting image? Why would a CADD system *not* be fully database-managed?

- Is the hardcopy output from the CADD system a true reproduction of the database and displayed image? Is it in the office's standard size and format? Is the plotted output both equal in quality to that of manual procedures and workable for last-minute revisions and additions? Do the peripheral hardcopy output devices perform all functions necessary to replicate the software commands?

- Have "best-way" procedures been implemented by the key operator in order to avoid consuming unnecessary time and creating undue mistakes? Have log-on procedures been streamlined? Have layer-sharing and layer-saving methods been established? Have common-function macros been added to the user-definable menu?

- Are training or retraining and upgrading programs in place or being planned to introduce new operators to the CADD system and to anticipate new and additional workstations?

- Has a service bureau phaseout procedure been established to allow easy transition to the (preferred) "on-your-own" condition? Can the service bureau be retained later for "overflow" drafting and workstation time?

- Is there a confident backup file system in place, and being consistently used, that allows both input to and output from file as required for all projects? How is the system's security being maintained?

- What is the active program for integrating reprographics into both data-input uses and hardcopy-handling efforts? Is the end result being considered before starting an active CADD drawing file? Do multiple plotting format "handshakes" exist? Can separate plot-spool formats be created if required?

- Have the project's material specifications been included in and integrated with the database management system? With this as a basis, have office design and drafting standards been initiated? Have they been reinforced with CADD system prompts and functional macros, to assure image and annotation compliance?

Final output

Anticipating the requirements set forth in Chapters 3 and 5, start a preliminary review of CADD system output by considering each item in Figure 2.11. Answer each item with a hard YES or NO (not now) response.

If YES, the output function is required, proceed to list each specific attribute required. For example the display terminal is a required output device, but it must (must not) be full-color rather than monochrome, and the terminal should have sufficient on-board ROM and random-access memory (RAM) to support local image processing. If the response is NO, list the reasons why the item will not be a part of the (initial) system. Negative reasons can include lack of finances, lack of space, and simply no need for that function.

2.3 Minimal Investment Package plus Upgrade

A properly functioning CADD system is an investment that is rather permanent. As shown in Section 1.3, the initial CADD system and workstation is an investment on the order of a new employee. However,

Should the CADD system have:	Yes	No
• Display terminal (color monitor-CRT)?	___	___
• Letter-quality printing?	___	___
• Ink-on-film pen plotting?	___	___
• Ink-on-paper pen plotting?	___	___
• Color ink-jet plotting?	___	___
• Black-and-white electrostatic plotting?	___	___
• Color electrostatic plotting?	___	___
• Photoplotting?	___	___
• Electron beam recording devices?	___	___
• Laser imaging?	___	___
• Computer output to microfilm (COM)?	___	___
• Hard-disk memory peripherals?	___	___
• Streaming tape drives?	___	___
• Modem interconnects to offline systems?	___	___
• Coordination with other project (manual) hardcopy?	___	___

Figure 2.11 Action list for CADD output needs.

the ROI may not be as quickly achieved in the short term with the artificially intelligent CADD as with the more truly intelligent human employee.

In that a CADD system can provide a very positive return over the long term, it must be considered as having a longer tenure than the average employee. Note that although use of the system for a minimum of 6 months is usually required before a true payback on the CADD investment begins, operator proficiency should begin within 2 months.

With computer systems improving and adding newer, and less expensive, upgrades about every 6 months, the long-term use of a CADD system must provide for these system upgrades. If the next, "improved" model of a particular CADD system, or the next functional level—from micro to mini, or mini to mainframe—is not compatible with the in-place CADD system, then a major long-term advantage will have been lost.

Minimum package

For some firms the move into computer-aided design and drafting is, in the first stage, simply a move into computers from a position of having a nonelectronic office. From this standpoint, as depicted in Figure 2.12, the minimal computer system should be able to handle word processing and (spreadsheet) data processing with its necessary output. The next stage would add graphics handling and output ca-

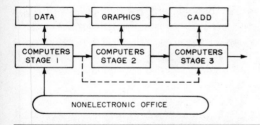

Figure 2.12 Staged entry into computers.

pabilities to the in-place computer system. Then the third stage would allow acquisition of CADD software. The dotted line in the figure denotes the end-run condition normally found when firms jump directly into implementation of CADD.

A computer system that is being acquired by a design and drafting office should provide for multifunctional use. For it to be able to accomplish only CADD functions would not be the most efficient use of the investment. Thus a minimal investment in a computer system *which is intended also to support CADD software* should have at least the elements listed in Figure 2.13.

Incredible as it may seem, this minimum single, high-quality CADD workstation system can be given a run for its money by an even smaller system. For approximately $6000, the elegant little Macintosh computer can be loaded with a simple CADD software program and linked with

---

1. Necessary software
   a. Word processing
   b. Spreadsheet
   c. File and database manager
   d. Compatible CADD system, 2-D only

2. Necessary hardware
   a. Any current, quality, 16-bit microcomputer CPU with two floppy-disk drives or one floppy drive plus an internal hard-disk system
   b. UNIX or MS-DOS operating system
   c. 512K RAM
   d. Keyboard
   e. Color monitor, eight-color, 1024x1024 CRT resolution
   f. Thumb wheels or joystick or mouse for cursor control
   g. 20-megabyte external hard-disk system
   h. Backup disks (hard or floppy)
   i. All required connectors

3. Necessary peripherals
   a. Letter-size dot matrix printer
   b. A0 (E) size multipen plotter

4. Necessary financing
   a. Approximately $25,000 minimum, plus training

Figure 2.13 Minimum requirements for one CADD workstation.

a dot matrix printer. This ultraminimal system can produce approximately 75 percent as much as the typical microcomputer system produces, but without the memory capacity and without the normal processing speed.

First upgrade

Figure 2.14 lists the expected upgrade packages that are often the first to be added to initial system installations. As the operator or operators become used to the CADD system, the pressure builds to acquire additional memory and additional software capability. The next request is for a second terminal which, for the microsystems, may best be handled as a stand-alone, or separate, complete workstation which would share existing backup systems and peripherals.

2.4 Capital Investment versus Service Bureau

One basic choice between options is available to potential CADD system users. Rather than investing in their own system, some firms have sought to lease the necessary CADD systems and services.

A firm may not be able to acquire a CADD system large enough to suit its needs for financial reasons or because of a short-term demand prospect. Or it often happens that the affordable and available quality CADD system may prove to be technologically out of date too soon after purchase. This point may leave a firm wanting, perceivably needing,

1. Additional* software
    e. Database management
    f. Compatible three-dimensional CADD system

2. Additional* hardware
    j. 512K RAM or 1.5M RAM
    k. Complete second 16-bit microcomputer workstation
    l. A0 (E) size digitizer board
    m. Backup disks (hard or floppy)
    n. All required connectors

3. Additional* peripherals
    c. Letter-size ink-jet color printer

4. Additional* financing
    b. Approximately $10,000 minimum plus training

    * Use this list in conjunction with Figure 2.13.

Figure 2.14 First upgrade to a CADD system.

the newer system but without the financial resources to acquire it (because of a prior commitment to the current system).

The investment path is often the preferable method for overall tax reasons, provided current financial resources can handle the down payment and related up-front expenses. Leasing of CADD systems entirely, or just in terms of online hours of rental, can be directly expensed or passed through to ultimate payees, providing current cash flow can handle the financial burden.

Leasing of a CADD system from a service bureau should include some value-added services from the service bureau. System installation and the time it takes to come up to speed should be greatly reduced, relative to learning from the system supplier's manuals. With capital investment in the hands of the service bureau, it will be the bureau that must stay up to date to satisfy the demands of clients.

The bottom line is that a microcomputer CADD system investment would be written off the books within 3 years. If the system started to pay back after 6 months, it is conceivable that after 2 years in operation with CADD, a firm might elect to analyze what the next CADD system would be and plan for its acquisition. The old system could then be given to a school or other charitable institution, although the firm would retain the generated database.

If the service bureau option is chosen, in order to acquire a larger number of workstations sooner and with greater software power, then an even greater emphasis will be placed on who is selected to operate the equipment and what project or projects will be placed online. There will be precious little time in which to accomplish the preliminary document planning so that the best use is made of the leased system. After all, the clock starts running upon delivery of the system (after start-up training) and the service bureau will insist upon being paid— just as the friendly banker does.

2.5 Evaluation of Personnel Training Programs

Everyone is involved when a CADD system becomes part of the design and drafting team, not just the system operators. Just as the key system operator or operators must be trained in depth concerning the CADD system's hardware and software, so also the general staff at a firm should be made familiar with the principal aspects of the new team member.

The prioritized list of personnel who should be trained in the use and capabilities of CADD is shown in Figure 2.15. One person should be selected as the system specialist, the in-house expert. This key operator or CADD manager should be made aware of all aspects of the CADD system's hardware and software. This person need not be the only one

FIRST LEVEL:	Key CADD operator System manager
SECOND LEVEL:	System operators CADD staff Project personnel
THIRD LEVEL:	Office staff Pertinent clients
FOURTH LEVEL:	Continuing education

Figure 2.15 Prioritized CADD training program levels.

who operates the system but should be the only one to set security functions and to interface with the system supplier, vendor, or service bureau.

The key operator should be the person to train or assist in training all other members of the CADD team and the office in general. At each level away from the key operator, less and less of the specifics of the CADD system's operation needs to be known. However, everyone should be made acquainted with how the CADD system will assist in producing the firm's projects.

Training for the key personnel should consist of at least three parts. First, hardware is the first and the last thing to be literally touched on a CADD system, and hence hardware is the first subject that is covered. How the system is powered up, how use of software is initiated, and how the system is shut down are very important, as are the methods of normal operation and filing.

The second and most lengthy training effort deals with the operating system and various software programs. Each operating system and software set has specific nuances which must be understood. Regardless of the training program offered by the vendor, it may be wise for each trainee to take an existing design document from his or her firm and generate a copy on the CADD system. This procedure should test both the system and the success of the training methods.

The third part of the training program never ends. It corresponds to the fourth level noted in Figure 2.15, continuing education. Just about the time one has mastered the system's software, new upgrades are added or new applications are created, thus entailing renewed training for familiarity and for new applications.

Design Process Impact: CADD Input Managing

Project application management of interactive computer graphic systems is independent of specific computer-aided design and drafting systems. First there is the design process itself—to which the multifaceted and interactive computer graphic systems can be properly applied. Whether enhanced or hindered by the introduction of CADD, the result or output from the design process is still of primary importance. Hence a CADD system must support and augment the design process.

This chapter considers CAD as design output and CADD as plotted hardcopy output at each phase of the design process. What is the interface between CADD and what is not CADD on the same project? How is CADD layering logic implemented for drawing and materials management? Where is the control over real-time use and ROI in CADD?

Budget approval

The preliminary answers to the above questions were established in Chapters 1 and 2. To assure greater clarity in assessing the impact of interactive graphics, set aside, for the moment, considerations of the costs of CADD systems. Consider that you already have an annualized, approved budget of $30,000 for a microcomputer system or as much as $500,000 for a very substantial mini-mainframe system. Also set aside the problems of workforce and space requirements. Consider that all the acquisition hassles are out of the way.

You have selected and purchased a CADD system. Now, plug in the system and bring it up to speed. Set aside the worries about reading the system manuals and finding the time for training. Think of all that as being completed. By considering how to best use this new design and drafting tool, different acquisition and training objectives may be highlighted. Ask the basic question: What are you going to do on it or with it first?

Input, then output

Once a commitment is made to the acquisition and application of a CADD interactive graphic system, several primary questions must be answered and the responses then adhered to in terms of your company's design and production goals. Where in the design and production process will this very versatile equipment system be applied? Will the application be limited to one phase of the design or production process, or will it be applied to several phases? Will the CADD system be used completely from start to finish throughout the process? Most important, what is to be the return on investment in this CADD system, and how will this ROI be determined?

First consider a project's design process as a simple input-work-output equation, and *only then* add a computer-aided design and drafting system into the mix. From this frame of reference, CADD usage is certainly not the final answer, by itself, to all design and production needs. It is, however, a most viable and worthwhile tool provided that the investment can be shown to have a positive return.

As is well known in practice and as discussed in numerous articles and books, CADesign and CADrafting systems will do exceptional work in a very rapid time frame. However, the CADD system that is now, or is yet to be, installed in your office must first receive data and drawings input which it then can work with to provide useful output pertinent to its application.[S1, S2]

Figure 3.1 shows the basic input-work-output equation which must be satisfied at each application point. The nature of the input will vary at each point, and the output type will vary based upon particular need. Perhaps the CADD system can be viewed as a new "employee" to whom instructions must be given and from whom drawings-as-output must flow in order for those drawings to be delivered to the client so that the professional services can be paid for.

Acquisition of a CADD system may force members of a firm to reconsider all their fundamental notions of how to approach a project, how to resolve it, how to properly show alternatives to the client, how to best create the hardcopy output, and then, how to reproduce that output. This review of design-to-production methods essentially requires applying the *logical sequence methods* of computer-assisted interactive graphics to the conventional design process.

This reanalysis may force the consideration of the project as a whole rather than only looking at the project from a "Do this step, then do next step" basis. Certainly the CADD implementation time frame and learning curve would be much longer without prior use of logical methods. Achieving the higher levels of productivity with CADD demands close project management control.

3.1 Design Process Impact Points

Just as each design project must be addressed along well-established lines of step-by-step analysis and known procedures, so also the application of CADesign, CADrafting, and CADD must adhere to these same criteria. At each step in the design process, the output productivity of CAD as a design function and CADD as a design and drafting function must be examined.

Production output at every point in the design process becomes input to the next process step. If the form of that previous output is incomplete or incompatible as input, then the next process activity may require unnecessary additional work or at worst be wholly negated (refer to Chapters 5 and 6).

The generalized aspects of any design process have been clearly delineated by K. Lonberg-Holm and C. Theodore Larson in their *Development Index.*[B4] Their analysis reduced the pattern and cycle of the basic design-development-use format to six phases:

1. Research   or   analysis

2. Design   or   synthesis

3. Production   or   formation

4. Distribution or   dispersion

5. Utilization   or   performance

6. Elimination   or   termination

Figure 3.3 delineates this cycle of development and prepares the logic format for the design-drafting cycle. These primal forms are echoed in the standard engineering and architectural design processes shown in Figure 3.3 as: (1) programming or schematic design phase, (2) functional relationships or preliminary design phase, (3) systems layout or design

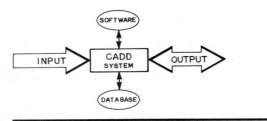

Figure 3.1 Input, then CADD, then output.

development phase, (4) working drawings, construction-fabrication drawings, or contact documents phase, (5) actual fabrication or construction phase, and (6) facility use or product application phase.

The output efficiency of the drawings, or hardcopy production, at each of these points varies with regard to their respective amounts of hand drafting or CADD applications. Refer to Chapter 5 for specific techniques for handling hardcopy output.

This open-ended, circular-flow reasoning is flattened out in Figure 3.4 to show the process as a linear flow. Viewed as a part of the fast-track charting process, this linear flow represents the main line for the standard manufacturing, engineering, and architectural design processes.[B5] The process sequence descriptions on top of the main flow line use the general terminology for the architect-engineer-contractor (AEC) community. The process terminology below the main line relates more to the manufacturing, design engineering, and fabrication industries.[B6]

Parallel with the fabrication-construction sequence is the line for shop drawings (or yard drawings) and the special cases of numerical control (NC) and robotics. Vital feedback in the traditional design process comes in the form of these manufacturers' and contractors' shop drawings of the actual or close-referenced "as-built" conditions. Finite size changes, alternate equipment installations, and construction or fabrication "hits" rectified by field, shop, or yard changes, occurs as a result of this contract-production process, involving documents, output, and review.

These revisions then return as new input to the initial contract documents. This feedback or input can cause further revisions and alterations which return later as the next output: design addenda and revision issues of the contract-production documents.

Whether or not these design process steps are required by a particular office, they represent what in fact is actually being pursued.

Reprographics production work flow

Before the application of CADD systems, the maximized production techniques for design and construction or fabrication drawings centered

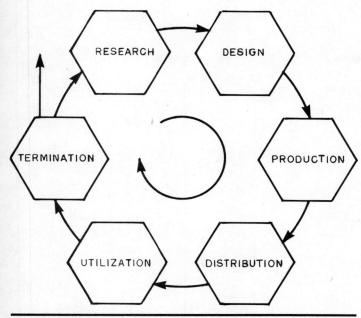

Figure 3.2   Cycle of development.

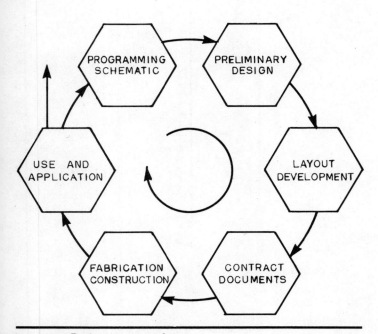

Figure 3.3   Design process cycle.

Figure 3.4 Design process linear flow.

on the use of hand drafting, assisted by reprographics techniques. These drafting systems utilized a mix of quality and quick hand-drafting methods with simple and complex reproduction techniques to generate drawings which communicated the design intent without burdening the designer with tedious and excessive redrafting.

For conventional and systems drafting, different reproduction techniques were applied at each phase of the design process, depending upon the graphic output desired. These reprographic techniques are still in wide use in support of CADD output and manual output, both as in-house functions and as supplied by contract from outside repro service firms.[B7, B8, B9] Figure 3.5 expands upon the linear chart of the design process to include these pre-CADD concepts.

By traditional methods, program analysis of the design often requires the use of existing documents that usually occur in a copy form which may not be easily reusable and must therefore be restored to a more reproducible or workable medium. Similarly, during the preliminary design synthesis, physical development, and early construction communication phases, certain drawings showing existing conditions may require restoration using reprographics techniques. In the realm of CADD systems, this restoration of existing data occurs during the digitizing function.

Related to photorestoration, electrostatic restoration, and scanning-digitizing is the en masse recapture of existing data using *photodrafting.* Actual continuous-tone, black-and-white photographic positives are incorporated into the project documents with this systems drafting method. Except for very large CADD systems, the pixel count and memory requirements of this form normally preclude databases consisting of complete or even partial photographs.

When preliminary design and concept development change over to detail design and system verification, many of the details and subsystems of previous project designs can be reused in part, if not in their entirety. Once captured within the system, whether by photorestoration, hand drafting, or digitizing for CADD, these detail components can be easily modified, replicated, reproduced, and used again to suit the new project's needs.

In the reprographics portion of design-production work flow, this reuse activity has the general name *copy, cut, and tape* which describes the actual process better than the more traditional title "pasteup drafting." In the CADD process, this type of activity can be labeled as similar to the word processing function of replication, relocation, and reformatting.

The subset of reprographics known as pin graphics, or *pin-registered overlay drafting,* is that layered systems drafting function done by hand which most closely matches the layered systems logic accomplished by

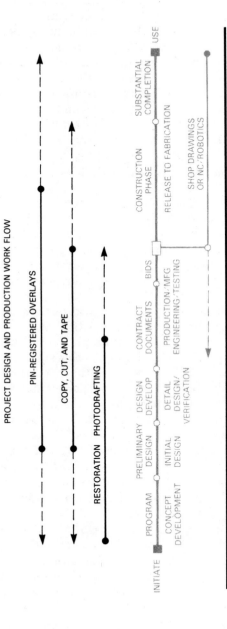

Figure 3.5 Reprographics in the design process.

the CADD interactive graphics process.The basis of overlay drafting is the sharing of the common-base background image as a layer separate from any particular discipline's description of their respective elements of that common background.[B7]

Physically registered overlay drafting is a graphic arts concept. It is used in the architectural, engineering, and manufacturing fields in much the same way as CADesign, CADrafting, and CADD. Graphic images and alphanumerics are mixed and separated onto reference and active layers to suit the various design elements, using interactive graphic and annotation software programs.

It is not in the province of this book to give definitive discussions of these reprographic techniques. Rather, the intent here is simply to show their correlation and similarity of purpose during the design-production process and as they relate to computer-aided systems.

For a thorough review of pin-registered overlay drafting, read the *Pin Graphics Manual,*[B7] which will also give an overview of layered systems logic. General reprographics and systems drafting procedures are also covered and further developed in *Unigrafs*[B8] and in *Systems Drafting.*[B9]

Computer-aided production work flow

When applying the logic and productivity of computer-aided design, engineering, and drafting to the main track of the design-construct process, each aspect must be analyzed separately. The impact of computer-aided *design* does not apply to production output in quite the same manner as it applies to computer-aided *engineering, testing,* or *manufacturing.* And what is initialized as an interactive computer-aided function in the design process is entirely different from a computerized aid in the drafting process.

For example, CADesign input, interaction, and output during design may be three-dimensional, with solids-modeling functions and displayed via CRT only. The output from CADD, on the other hand, is normally an interactive two-dimensional function with display both on a terminal monitor CRT and as a hardcopy plot by electrostatics; or as a pen plot onto paper or film; or as a photoplot to microfilm, videotape, or slides.

Consider the linear flow of the design process (first shown in Figure 3.4) as it is now interactively assisted by the several computerized graphic functions. Figure 3.6 provides an overview of these CADD processes and also shows their primary activities and alternate use areas. For a mixing of the reprographic drafting systems with CADD capabilities, Chapter 7 provides an extensive discussion of CADD as a repligraphic drafting system. This current figure should not be construed as showing CADD and its subfunctions as stand-alone entities. In all cases, CADD is seen to be a design and drafting tool which works in conjunction with numerous other techniques.

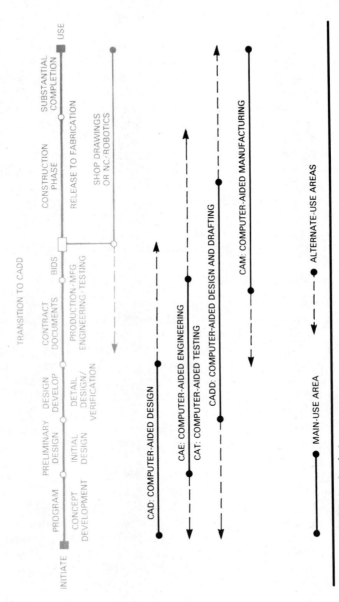

Figure 3.6 CADD in the design process.

Design with CADD

In engineering and architectural systems the initial programming or schematic design phase finds a direct use for CADesign—computer-aided design. For manufacturing and industrial design areas, this initial realm is referred to as the "conceptual development phase." In both cases the primary function is to analyze alternate configurations of the basic requirements, the raw data, and the client's needs. CADesign systems output may normally appear as a display via the CRT only, for there may not necessarily be a need for a separate hardcopy.

CADesign serves as a superior tool in the collection of data, the ready-access filing of that data, and the manipulation of that data for schematic and concept analysis, *provided that a clear and responsive database management system is included in the interactive package.*

The initial CADesign and database program analysis can become the basis for preliminary or initial design configuration layouts—a drafting function. What may have started out before CADesign as hand-drafting or photographic recapturing of existing data (with multiple retracing and recopying for alternate schemes), is now merely recalled or re-addressed from the reference database and displayed for review and further delineation on the terminal's CRT.

Not only are data representations available by CADesign in three dimensions, with precise tolerances for early checking of major systems integrations and interferences, but also the presentation of multiple heretofore cost-prohibitive "what-if" schemes can be easily achieved without losing, redrawing, or harming the primary database. This can be achieved while still maintaining a record of each of the "what-ifs" for future use.

The above references to a complete and functioning database management system with three-dimensional wire-frame and solids-modeling packages imply that thorough applications of the principles and guidelines of Chapter 2 have been undertaken. As each step of the project-design work-flow process develops, the application of CADesign, CADrafting, CADD, or even the high-level production efficiency of hand-drafting repro systems is determined by considering the impact of each method on the next stage in the process.

Engineering with CADD

Figure 3.6 further shows that, when the CADesign function moves from program analysis to preliminary design, its imagery could and should be shared. Can the computer-aided engineering (CAE) function utilize the same project database?

A distinction needs to be made at this juncture between CAE for architectural facilities and industrial manufacturing engineering and

CAE for electronics and printed circuit board design, engineering, and layout. Although many of the layering logic systems and functional applications are similar, this book deals primarily with architectural and industrial uses, not with circuit design.

As a design develops into a more formal delineation of shape and size, the CADesign imagery should specifically lend itself to CAE for *finite element analysis* (FEA) methods.[A3] Both CADesign and CAE/FEA, which require three-dimensional handling and color imaging, must become the basis for the two-dimensional representation of the design via CADD. These two-dimensional drawings are the construction documents or production manufacturing engineering and fabrication sheets that, as hardcopy, carry the design function off the system and into the real world.

Feedback from CAE to CADesign may come in the form of physical modeling and system testing of the design. Here the CAE design function may be further delineated as *computer aided testing* (CAT) which can return systemwide design data modifications. Changes may be discreet revisions to the finite element data on the design side of CADD, which then calls for another round of the CAE and CADD drafting functions. And hence again through as many iterations of the process as are required.

Computer-aided engineering and its in-depth design analysis functions may often be only digital or alphanumeric functions, with output as printed sheets of data. Graphic display of the massaged data to a monitor CRT can be included for interactive engineering. In this case, there may be separate and distinct wire-frame, surface texture, and color-equals-stress graphic images which are used for analysis but are not to be drawn in plotted hardcopy as a part of the basic production package. CAE systems output may be softcopy upgrades to the design database, alphanumeric hardcopy printouts, or even COM microfiche of stress curve diagrams and calculations for filing purposes.

Design and drafting with CADD

At the contract documents juncture, the CADesign function in Figure 3.6 gives way to the more output-oriented computer-aided design and drafting. Output now is in anticipation of the release of contract drawings for bid purposes or as a direct release for fabrication. The primary activities in this phase are hardcopy drafting–oriented. However, as the project continues to be more precisely delineated, design alternatives are constantly being considered. Hence, the term "CADD" is correctly applied to simultaneous design and drafting functions.

Release for fabrication may be in the form of engineering arrangement and systems-design schematic and isometric, two-dimensional drawings.

Release of bids before a contract is signed for construction in the architectural or engineering mode usually entails a high volume of copies in tangible hardcopy form rather than only electromagnetics (softcopy output).

Note in Figure 3.6 that the alternate-use areas for CADD extend from the start of the design process to design development, then reappear in midconstruction or midfabrication, and continue through to the end of the production process. The main-use area is most correctly related to the traditional drafting or hardcopy mode: contract and fabrication documents. However, CADD is also often used as a catchall phrase for all the various methods and systems of interactive computer-aided graphics.

When integrated with a relational database management system that allows multiple attributes to be attached to the CADD graphics and text, this CADD function may best be used as a true computer-aided facilities management (CAFM) system.[A8, A9] Once a design has been developed and put into use, maintenance and continued control of the facility or assembly are a viable outcome of the use of CADD. The database can remain active; it need not be permanently filed.

Manufacturing and CADD

The next line or track computer-aided manufacturing (CAM) represents a much higher degree of three-dimensional design, solids modeling, and FEA methods. CAM requires design input with a fully augmented and well-managed database to allow report writing, materials takeoff summaries, and perpetual inventory analysis and control in order to design, fabricate, distribute, track, or control production. Drawings are usually initiated in two dimensions; the resultant images are then used as a basis for generating the three-dimensional imagery in wire-frame, surface, and solids modeling.

One current term for this seemingly all-inclusive use of computers in manufacturing is computer-integrated manufacturing (CIM). In the case of CIM, the highly productive concepts of materials resource planning (MRP) are an integral part of CADD's relational database management procedures.

This computer-augmented method is often used in the combination CAD/CAM, where the output from the CADesign function is linked directly to the CAM function, bypassing many of the intermediate drafting and plotting steps. Output may be direct via softcopy, in purely electromagnetic form, for tape-driven fabrication using *numerical control* and *robotics.* For the most part, this CAD/CAM form of computer-aided interactive graphics applies primarily to precision manufacturing and not to the typical AEC facilities design and construction.

Impact of repligraphics

For whichever design process method is pursued, reprographics or CADD (or the combination of reprographics and CADD known as "repligraphics"), a major watershed is crossed when the scope of work changes from design and drafting to construct or fabricate. Figure 3.7 shows the manual techniques of reprographics and the manual-plus-electronic methods of CADD jointly paralleling the main track of the design process.

Take the rapid *replic*ation of an integrated database image and join it with the hardcopy output capabilities of repro*graphics,* and the net result is maximized production *repligraphics.* By combining the fastest aspects of CADD, replication, and quick redrafting (replotting) with the advanced techniques of production reprographics, repligraphics maximizes the multiple use and reuse of the design communication images.[A10] Refer to Chapter 7 for the practical applications of repligraphics for CADD hardcopy output.

As further discussed in Chapters 5 and 6, the hardcopy output for a design project starts to be the primary goal at the outset of the contract or fabrication documents phase. All during preliminary design and detail design and verification, hardcopy presentations are secondary to the design process. Too much of the design is still in flux during those preliminary stages, and only partial scope-development records and checksets (checkplots in hardcopy) are required.

At the point of bids or release for fabrication, the drafted and plotted hardcopy output must communicate the design concept to the third party. All the aforementioned CAD/CAE/CADD/CAM or hand-drafted reprographics systems are invalid if they do not provide legible, logical design communications to the fabricator or constructor.

CADD filing with micrographics

Depending upon the nature of the construction or fabrication process (whether traditional manufacturing and construction practices or the advanced NC and robotics-directed systems are used), there is either a vast amount of plotted two-dimensional hardcopy to be generated and filed, a database to be maintained and filed, or a COM or other micrographics system reference to be considered.

This bottom-line record-keeping function in a computer-aided, interactive design system may best be kept as a form of micrographics known as computer output to microfilm (COM). Figure 3.8 adds COM as the bottom line to the design process linear flow.[S1, S2, S3]

As the project-design and production work-flow process nears its ultimate purpose, that of providing an item, system, or facility for use

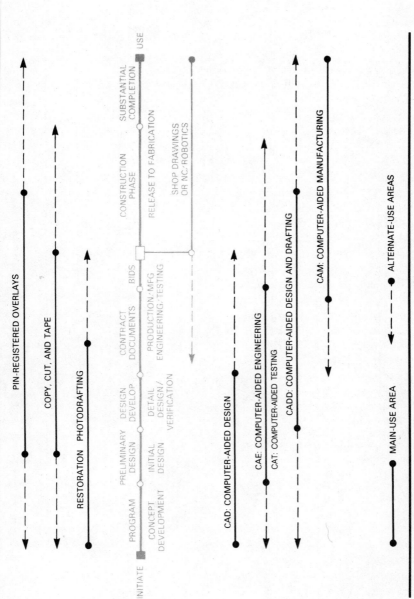

Figure 3.7 Repligraphics in the design process.

PROJECT DESIGN AND PRODUCTION WORK FLOW

PIN-REGISTERED OVERLAYS

COPY, CUT, AND TAPE

RESTORATION   PHOTODRAFTING

INITIATE

PROGRAM

CONCEPT
DEVELOPMENT

PRELIMINARY
DESIGN

INITIAL
DESIGN

DESIGN
DEVELOP

DETAIL
DESIGN/
VERIFICATION

CONTRACT
DOCUMENTS

PRODUCTION, MFG
ENGINEERING, TESTING

BIDS

CONSTRUCTION
PHASE

RELEASE TO FABRICATION

SHOP DRAWINGS
OR N.C. ROBOTICS

SUBSTANTIAL
COMPLETION

USE

CAD: COMPUTER-AIDED DESIGN

CAE: COMPUTER-AIDED ENGINEERING

CAT: COMPUTER-AIDED TESTING

CADD: COMPUTER-AIDED DESIGN AND DRAFTING

CAM: COMPUTER-AIDED MANUFACTURING

● MAIN-USE AREA

●——— ALTERNATE-USE AREAS

57

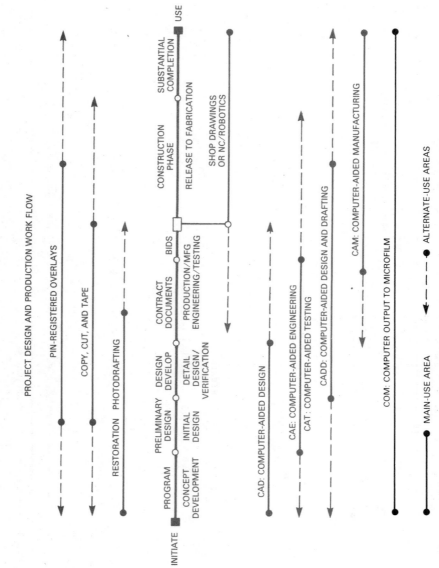

PROJECT DESIGN AND PRODUCTION WORK FLOW

PIN-REGISTERED OVERLAYS

COPY, CUT, AND TAPE

RESTORATION   PHOTODRAFTING

INITIATE

PROGRAM   PRELIMINARY   DESIGN   CONTRACT   CONSTRUCTION   SUBSTANTIAL   USE
CONCEPT   DESIGN   DEVELOP   DOCUMENTS   PHASE   COMPLETION
DEVELOPMENT INITIAL   BIDS
            DESIGN   DETAIL   RELEASE TO FABRICATION
                          DESIGN/
                          VERIFICATION
                                    PRODUCTION/MFG
                                    ENGINEERING/TESTING

SHOP DRAWINGS
OR NC/ROBOTICS

CAD: COMPUTER-AIDED DESIGN

CAE: COMPUTER-AIDED ENGINEERING

CAT: COMPUTER-AIDED TESTING

CADD: COMPUTER-AIDED DESIGN AND DRAFTING

CAM: COMPUTER-AIDED MANUFACTURING

COM: COMPUTER OUTPUT TO MICROFILM

●——————● MAIN-USE AREA

◀---- ---- ---▶ ● ALTERNATE-USE AREAS

Figure 3.8 COM as a file and audit trail.

58

as designed, it is useful to look back over the process for an audit trail. The audit trail is a record of how the initial need was developed into a viable design and then constructed or manufactured according to some accepted standard tolerances and specifications.

COM can be the principal hardcopy filing system for computer-aided design, engineering, drafting, and manufacturing. Aside from the softcopy output onto disk and tape, output via COM methods provides an efficient, remote, and relatively secure, though offline, hardcopy of the database product. With the aid of photoprojection techniques, COM can avoid many of the hassles of full-scale image plotting and replotting.

A secondary file by electromagnetic disk or tape storage may be kept, ostensibly for ease of recalling images to active status as part of a particular future database. But softcopy cannot be relied upon for archival quality because of the possibility of demagnetization, and even laser-imaged records can be damaged. Micrographics techniques usually are the most efficient way of filing all the hardcopy documents.

Conventional projects using manual and systems drafting, and indeed also CADD systems, require keeping a hardcopy file of each significant point in the scope of the project. Records of design calculations, whether by hand or by a computer *electronic data processing* (EDP) device, should correlate with the early CADesign and CAE as well as encompass the CADD-plotted output and the CAD/CAM machine control directives.

Impact synopsis

Thus, as shown in the design-process flow figures in this section, the cycle of design-development-use (see Figure 3.1) returns in spiral fashion, not just in linear fashion but also full-circle, offset by time. The COM hardcopy or data disk or tape file becomes the database for subsequent research and analysis for the next design project, and the active database can continue to help manage the ongoing facility or project.

In examining the points of impact by CADD on the production design process flow, and when correlated with hand-drafting production, the widest justifiable applications of CADD can be appreciated. But a YES/NO logic gate approach to each application impact point must be considered before CAD/CAE/CADD/CAM/COM is implemented or any aspect of the hand-drafting methods is abandoned.

The synergistic applications of CADesign and CADrafting and hand-drafting reprographics or repligraphics, when properly applied at each of the six design phases delineated here and in the *Development Index,*[B4] give back a return on investment far in excess of that ROI obtainable by any one method alone. However, the process must be logically planned and executed.[B6]

3.2   Application Justification at Impact Points

As delineated in Section 3.1, the transition-to-CADD scenario must be considered at each point in the design-production process. Similarly, in the acquisition of a CAD/CAE/CADD/CAM/COM system, certain anticipated functions will dictate the procedures and methods used in obtaining a computer-aided design and drafting workstation device or devices. Input capabilities and output needs at each point in the design process will be impacted by how CADD is applied.

Macroview of CADD input-output

Combining the line items in Figure 3.6 with the initial system-acquisition logic from Chapter 2 produces a single critical path diagram, shown in Figure 3.9. This maximum-angle overview of the CADD system's integration into the design process recognizes the ongoing design system demands and early training requirements. A secondary impact on system procurement is the initiation of the first-to-be-applied, specific design project.

After acquisition, design input with CAD, supported by a database management system and adequate operator training, allows highly productive CADD design and drafting output. On the database side, CADesign is supported by CAE in conjunction with whatever reference files and other available data can be readily accessed by the DBMS system. Consider for a moment: How will the existing drawing-files database be accessed into the new CADD system?

On the output side, CADesign can feed directly to CAM (CAD/CAM) and directly down the main line to CADD design and drafting. Or output can be indirectly to both via the database management system functions.

CADD output, in terms of hardcopy, goes directly to fabrication and construction or indirectly via bid documents and through the feedback loop of shop drawings. Ancillary output to and from CADD via project materials and design specifications criteria interacts with the database for continuity verification.

Similarly, materials resource planning and bills-of-materials (BOM) takeoffs are an interactive analysis function of the database management system.[B3, B10] This point could be called the heart and soul of a proper CADD system; without DBMS the true productivity of computer-aided interactive graphics will not be realized.

When the prototype or model is created from the design development stage in the CAD-to-CAM process, it can be directly tested and analyzed with computer-aided testing. This prototype testing further refines the design (CADesign) input so that CADD's output will better facilitate

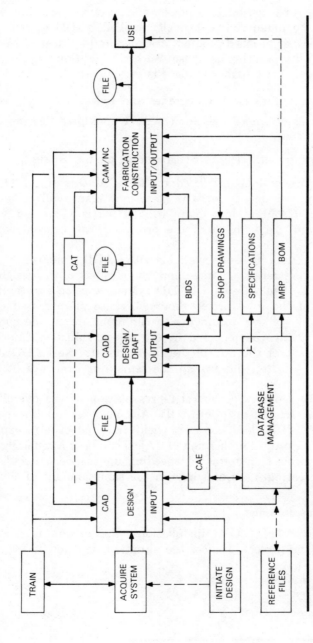

Figure 3.9 Macroview outline.

fabrication and assembly. This final production step is also properly labeled "input-output" since it reflects the feedback from shop design, critical path construction techniques, and resource planning.

It should be noted that a logically applied CADD system provides not only a proper finished product, designed and fabricated for effective use, but also the resulting database. With the additional option of finite element analysis, a CADD database is established for:

1. Retrieval for after-market upgrades and redesign

2. Retrieval as reference files for the next or related designs

3.3   Percentage and Types of Drawings on the System

What drawings will be produced on the CADD system? Of all the drawings and documents for a project, how many will be completely created with CADD? How many will be partially created using the CADD system? How much of the project design process will utilize CADD?

The productivity increases available with CADD systems can approach 1.5:1 or even greater, depending upon which aspect of the design process is considered. If full use of a CADD system were to save as much as 15 percent of the total project hours, because of increased efficiency and the ability of the documents to communicate the designs, where would this savings be reflected in the project? Just as important, if only 65 percent of the project drawings were to use CADD and they could be done faster, how would the remaining drawings fit into the time flow?

Figure 3.10 provides a general representation of the overall project time and the relative use of CADD. Although several instances have shown that CADD does not even yield 1:1 productivity, experienced users note that proper application of CADD can have a generally positive effect on a project in terms of speeding up the design and drafting process or creating more drawings in the same amount of time.

Percentage of drawings

In the majority of CADD installations, the system is not utilized throughout the project. Hence, the situation depicted in Figure 3.10,

Figure 3.10 Overall use of CADD.

although certainly achievable, should be considered in the specific application areas. The active sections of the design process generally overlap one another rather than being found as definitive cutoff points. That those portions of each design process section which use CADD systems will be completed up to 15 percent faster creates definite stresses at the overlap areas of these sections.

The percentage use of CADD on a typical project might be better demonstrated by a sequence, Figures 3.11, 3.12, and 3.13. For many firms the interactive graphics computer system is a design tool which is used only for the design aspects of a project. This situation requires that all CADD hardcopy output and project savings accrue to the programming and design budget, as depicted in Figure 3.11, with no appreciable direct effect on drafting of working drawings or on construction or fabrication.

If, as some firms claim, the interactive graphics computer system were primarily a drafting tool, its use would be restricted to the drafting areas: design development and contract documents. Figure 3.12 shows no percentage of design drawings using CADD, and thus any savings would accrue only to the contract documents budget.

Figure 3.13 may be closer to the current usage of computer-aided design and drafting systems in that both design functions and drafting functions receive the benefits of CADD's higher productivity. Yet if the CADD portion of the document set is only 65 percent, then what manual methods will be used to create the remaining 35 percent of the

Figure 3.11 Use of CADD in design.

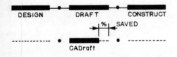

Figure 3.12 Use of CADD in drafting.

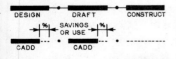

Figure 3.13 Use of CADD in design and drafting.

documents? Changing the ratio to 35 percent CADD with 65 percent manual causes a profound difference in what specific drawings actually use CADD.

To put it succinctly, what is the *first drawing* to use CADD on your project? What is the *first 10 percent of the set of project drawings?* Can the database that is created for the first drawing be used for subsequent drawings? What portion of the first 10 percent can be extended through the first 65 percent of the project documents? And so on.

Types of drawings

Refer again to Figure 2.10, and consider first those drawings that are for design purposes. Bear in mind that the "intelligence" of a computer is its ability to store information and then to rapidly process that information into the same or different configurations. With this frame of reference, the choice of proper drawing types becomes easier.

Concept and programming layouts become viable drawings that can be delivered in some form of hardcopy after the decision support work has been considered. Budget considerations, available resources, and the user's needs are articulated into graphic displays which usually require several alternatives to allow for full choices:

- Spatial blocking diagrams
- Flow diagrams
- Phase 1, phase 2, phase 3, . . . developments
- Tooling and standard tolerancing limits
- Adjacency layouts and flow patterns

The key to these first CADD images should be an understanding of which portions of the images can be used for next-stage developments. Portions of alternate concept sheets and sequential phasing drawings are used for each successive display. Elements of schematic flow diagrams and adjacency layouts are reused and redefined to suit differing arrangements. These design portions may be the best first use of a CADD system. Although it is the graphic image that is thought of as being shared, a thorough database management system can allow sharing of even more portions of the design.

Preliminary plans and details bring the initial design concepts and programming requirements up to a relatively firm level at which alternative planning at the major scope level has almost ceased. The initial design is hardening more into the specific direction that it will be taking. Standard detail elements and predetermined subsystems are now factored into the design:

- Basic plan modules
- Site footprints for alternate locations
- Forging blank limitations with machine limits
- Standard details and reusable component parts

Some of these drawings were built upon elements defined in earlier stages. Initial three-dimensional massing and modeling representations are included and flattened to two dimensions as required. Recurring modularity and components are selected for use in later drawing stages.

Presentation drawings capture the foregoing display and hardcopy drawings for submittal to reviewing authorities. Multiangle views, relationships in multicolor, and output in multimedia are the essence of presentation using CADD. The term "drawings" may not be appropriate since the forms of presentation may include:

- Direct displays and videotapes of preliminary plans
- Three-dimensional and perspective views of subassemblies and full assemblies
- Field fills in color denoting adjacent uses on slides
- Partial plots of selected portions at reduced scales

The accuracy and easily changed visual attributes of a CADD system are nowhere as useful as in its presentation functions. The apparently simple display to the terminal monitor is an exciting presentation in itself. Although monochrome displays and output can differentiate elements using a variety of line weights, text fonts, and field-fill descriptions, only polychrome, or full color, is worthy of complete presentation.

Design development and detail design verification drawings, when done in the conventional manual drafting modes, often redraw portions of the preliminary design concepts. CADD allows these next-stage development sheets to truly be verifications and in-depth continuances of the initial designs:

- Complete floor plans with basic dimensioning
- Cut and fill and vegetation layouts for site work
- Phased fabrication steps for assembly-line stages
- Nonformat detail plots for offline repligraphics

Following the lead of manual drafting with systems drafting techniques, this stage in design development actually can be 60 to 80 percent of the completed contract documents. There is no need to redraw or regenerate the database; it is in active file (with backups!). Hence all that is necessary is to continue to refine the design concepts and reuse the details.

Contract and production documents are the extension of the design development images. With CADD the time allotted to the contract construction or fabrication drawings portion of the design process is easily reduced by collapsing it into a majority of the design verification process portion. This area is primarily drafting, and CADD-the-drafter can achieve some of its greatest productivity during the myriad revision-recheck-redraw actions at this stage:

- Facility plans and schedules
- Orthographic views and isometrics
- Process flow diagrams and schematics
- Hidden databases of "intelligent drawings"

Because of the wealth of data generated with the CADD interactive graphic images, the normal concept of a drawing must be expanded to include the *hidden intelligence* behind the lines, curves, and text of the drawing. If just the visual image or plot is considered, much that is the true function of CADD may be lost or missed.

All types of drawings can and have been done with CADD systems. Duplicate drawing copies with only slight modifications to change the "story" of the image are done using CADD, without the redrafting onus of manual creation. But the CADD system should be looked upon as creating, rather than drawings per se, a database in which the traditional concept of drawings—a two-dimensional representation of the (future) three-dimensional object—merely acts as a method for providing differing hardcopy viewing angles of the database.

3.4 Interface between System Language and Consultants

If the creation of project documents for the purpose of fabricating or constructing some item or facility is changing from the creation of physical tracings and working drawings to the much more useful creation of an *intelligent database,* then the need will be to understand the language of the database. This language can be found, first, in the machine's operating system and, second, in the word and symbology usage of the CADD software program.

Take time to read the Glossary of terms at the back of this book. Then seek out the operator's manuals for the CADD system that you intend to purchase. The operator's manual for the hardware system should include a glossary and instructions concerning the disk operating system (DOS). There should also be a manual for the CADD software program that you intend to acquire.[B14] If these manuals are not available or are not easy to follow, perhaps you should consider another system.

An initial clarification of the terminology and graphic languages for your system will help the operators to have a better command of the hardware and software. However, just reading the glossary and user manuals will not prepare you completely for maximized use of the CADD system. Actually, too much reading of the "new languages," or new uses of old words and descriptive terms, may only serve to confuse rather than to enlighten.

Hands-on practice, not merely viewing a canned presentation, is the proper way to gain a working understanding of CADD terminology. Work with a *small group of picture elements* from one of your own drawings. Take the probe pen or puck in your hand, key in the command sequence with the other hand, and view the terminal's display monitor to determine how to properly move a set of intelligent lines from one layer to another. Then replicate the relocated data string and vectored graphics to new configurations and spool the sheet in a plot file for later despooling to a hardcopy device.

Using consultants

Your first line of defense for keeping your CADD system productive is to seek out and use the resources of the manufacturers and vendors of the hardware and software systems. This constitutes another checklist item for proper acquisition of a CADD system. If the local vendor of your potential CADD system does not have local or easily accessible consultants, consider another system which does.

The national offices of the major CADD software and turnkey systems normally have a software or customer support center, or both, with many true systems experts. Users' questions about specific problems and the subsequent answers may be, and usually are, incorporated into the next software upgrades. Thus users' feedback is built-in assistance that is necessary for long-term vendor and software excellence.

A certain level of consultancy and assistance with software and hardware upgrades is expected. Help over and beyond this simple necessity will probably have a fee requirement. Special and operation-specific assistance for CADD software situations will usually be expensive if good and if available from outside consultants.

Service bureaus, whose function is to provide CADD drafting and leasing services, are often a most viable source for software performance and hardware interface consultation. System leasing bureaus often pride themselves on value-added leases. Solutions to problem situations discovered by one lessee are immediately available to the remainder of the client base.

But the best consultant may be your own key operator. By learning the fundamentals of how your specific system responds to your specific needs, the key operator may be able to create shorthand solutions with macros and minute "tweaking" of your software. These solutions can be sold back up the ladder to the vendor or marketed to the public if the applications prove to be a generic resource.

Project team consultants

The other pertinent project consultants represent the specific disciplines that are necessary for the professional completion of the project. As consultants they are presupposed to be out-of-house, across town, or even in a different state. It would be proper for them to use the CADD database and hardcopy images for your project. Unfortunately, if they have any CADD system at all, it most often is not compatible with that of the lead discipline or the principal host computer.

Figure 3.14 outlines the basic relationship between the lead design discipline and the client for the purpose of bringing to fruition the project with the assistance of the contractor or fabricator. The lead discipline often requires the services of several outside (not in-house) consulting disciplines in order to properly complete the project documents. These project documents typically would travel along the connecting lines of communication: a network. Under conventional manual drafting measures, the consulting disciplines would share reproductions of the lead discipline's drawings. These same communications channels could share the CADD database if the systems were all compatible.

In Chapter 7, Figure 7.13 delineates the repligraphic methods for sharing pin-registered hardcopies, offline from the host computer system. Similarly, in Chapter 5 there are many references to the means and methods for sharing CADD hardcopy before the revision process, while still on-stream and after the CADD system has been released to another project.

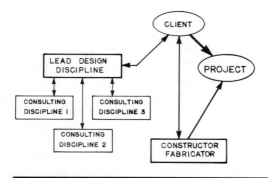

Figure 3.14 Project team.

Chapter

4

Layering Logic Control

In first applying a CADD system to existing design and production drafting procedures, it may be well to compare the logic sequence of conventional drawings production with the similar flow sequence for drawings produced by pin-registered overlays and CADD. This comparison of logic continuity follows the basic premise of taking an initial concept through design to drafting for production, with ultimate output as a constructed or fabricated facility, part, or assembly. (See Chapter 1, Section 1.1, and Chapter 3, Figure 3.4.)

Beginning with the left-hand column of Figure 4.1, conventional input for drafting and design methods starts with data input to a formatted sheet. This manually drawn image is then reproduced to allow for review and comments which feed back to the original drawing for revision and subsequent reprinting for further review. If the drawn image is shared by several disciplines, multiple copies are made which are in turn *manually drawn on* by the disciplines.

The review-comment-revision process then continues, compounded by the number of multiple shared-image disciplines involved. "Final" output then becomes the "final" reproduction prints which are dispersed as required for fabrication and construction.

The center column of Figure 4.1 traces the next logical flow path in the clear transition to CADD. This suggested intermediate step between

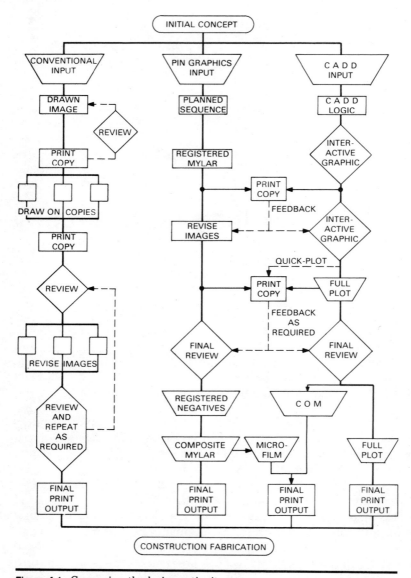

Figure 4.1 Comparing the logic continuity.

conventional drafting and computer-aided design and drafting is known as "pin-registered overlay drafting" (or "pin graphics").[B7]

Input to pin graphics utilizes all the techniques of hands-on conventional drafting but separates the shared and unique data onto distinct physical layers. These systems drafting procedures allow for the understanding, utilization, and proper application of layered systems drafting techniques. Pin-registered overlay drafting suggests that, for those images which will be shared on a project and for those common areas requiring constant revisions, hand drafting on separate but aligned layers will save tedious redrafting hours and dollars.

While the cost of pin graphics is from 1/1000 to 1/10,000 that of CADD systems, the procedures are similar and the resultant hardcopy output may even be more versatile (i.e., the use of screen tints and subordinate imaging is readily possible). What is not created here is the volatile and nonvolatile database for continued intra- and inter-project use.

Figure 4.1 delineates this image-from-description separation procedure as a part of a forced "planned-sequence" step that is valid for, but is often overlooked in, conventional systems. The planning step is necessary to determine shared base layers. Planning is also required to assure that the *output from each segment is compatible with and useful as input* to the succeeding process segment.

Rather than simple prints, pin-registered punched polyester matte and clear film layers are drawn on and photoreproduced or contact-reproduced to accommodate the review-comment-revision process. "Final" output is again contact-direct, or photoprojection hardcopy composites from reduced-size negatives of the various layers. Micrographics handling of the "final" output forms includes capturing only the composite images, not the individual layer images.

The CADD input column on the right-hand side in Figure 4.1 shows the similar forced, or required, logic step needed to determine the layer functions and the display, plot, or database analysis controls. Just as revisions to the shared layers in pin graphics need not be further nor redundantly revised by the related discipline users, so also with CADD. One of this interactive graphic system's logic methods is to share discrete layers or combinations of layers between several distinct, formatted sheets.[S1, S2, S3]

Lines, curves, and text are generated in the CADD database and displayed on the terminal monitor. Drafting is done electromagnetically for the first time, rather than manually. However, to obtain a checkprint, another electronic form must be utilized: a plotter must be instructed to recreate the database as an original in hardcopy form. This checkplot could be a thermographic "quick-look" copy of the CRT's display image for offline comments, or it could be a full plot.

Revisions to the CADD drawings are given as instructions to the database and are reflected in the updated monitor-CRT displays and in subsequent hardcopy checkplots. This feedback loop is finally closed when all disciplines sign off on the database before formal issuance of the project documents.

What is a draw-print-review-revise manual feedback loop for each conventional discipline drawing becomes a revise-discipline-only step in pin graphics. Further productivity is provided as the computer becomes the functional interactive graphic, shared-user-prompted electronic design and drafting medium.

"Final" CADD output is then in whatever form the fabrication and construction industries are currently demanding and using. Micrographics output might be directly in the form of COM or as microfilm copies of the plotted hardcopies. Softcopy output could be direct to robotics via NC.

4.1 Setup Rules and Examples of Project Drawings

Many items that we take for granted in manual and systems drafting methods require specific, planned directions in CADD systems. From the basic size of a sheet to the title block and border format, which is normally printed on the sheet, these "little things" and their tedious, minute details must be specifically addressed or user-defined in a CADD system.[B11] However, once these items are addressed, they can be reused forever unless a revision is required.

This permanence, and the normal difficulty in accessing the requisite commands, can be tyrannical; there is a latent hesitation about and difficulty in making any fundamental changes. But maybe that is OK— if you do not like making changes. Going deeply into software commands and operating system procedures requires attention to "housekeeping" duties which may seem tedious and certainly takes away from the real productivity of generating drawings.

What follows is a discussion of some basic rules for establishing sheet sizes and drawing formats. The procedures discussed are automatic, that is, buried deep in the programming, for some software programs. These rules *can* be acted upon in some programs, *must* be specifically set or accomplished for other systems, and under most circumstances *may not* be accessed, touched, or revised in a few CADD software programs. Use what you can, and do not worry too much about the remainder until you become expert with your system.

Sheet size

In the manual drafting realm, we can prepare to draw by taking a precut sheet of matte drafting film, translucent vellum, or bond paper from a storage file. The cut-sheet sizes are the standard A0 to A5 (E to A). For a CADD system, these standard sheet sizes may not be in place, or the CADD system may be set to handle sizes that are not your office standard sizes.[B7]

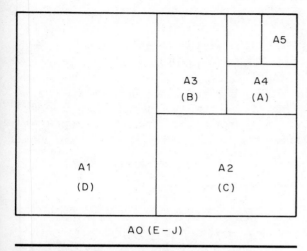

Figure 4.2 Standard sheet sizes—graphic.

For many CADD software programs, the monitor display image for a given sheet outlines the sheet as a dotted line around the perimeter of the CRT display. This dotted line normally represents the edge of the cut sheet for a particular sheet size. The dotted line may also be used to represent the hard-edge limits of a selected window.

Figure 4.2 provides a graphic representation of the assorted standard sheet sizes that are then tabulated in Figure 4.3. The definition of these sheet sizes, as a reusable symbol or as a dotted "trim-edge" line on the display, must be set for the specific drawing format. Note that whereas in manual drafting we would merely rotate a small-size sheet to provide either vertical or horizontal format, this distinction also must be formally set for CADD.

Metric code	Dimensions, millimeters (vertical x horizontal)	Conventional code	Dimensions, inches (vertical x horizontal)
	914.4x1219.2	J	36x48
A0	840.0x1188.0	E	30x42
A1	594.0x 840.0	D	24x36
A2	420.0x 594.0	C	18x24
A3	297.0x 420.0	B	11x17
A4h	210.0x 297.0	Ah	8.5x11
A4v	297.0x 210.0	Av	11x8.5
A5h	148.0x 210.0		
A5v	210.0x 148.0		

Figure 4.3 Standard sheet sizes tabulated.

Special attention must also be given to the metric and conventional (imperial) sheet-size dimensions. Some CADD software programs can be set to default to given sheet scales. If the metric sheet size is selected, the default would be to the metric scale (preset as "cm" for centimeters or "mm" for millimeters). If the conventional sheet size is chosen, the imperial scale of feet and inches is normally set (the default scale is often in ″ for inches). These selections must be made. Occasionally there may be some difficulty in attempting to incorporate macroplanning scale-control features such as yards, miles, meters, and kilometers when the defaults are in inches or millimeters.

Sheet format

In a CADD system the title block and border format of a drawing is not preprinted, nor is it usually previously installed in the software. The format lines must be generated to suit the sheet sizes and corresponding scales. If hardcopy plotting is to be done using preprinted formats, then at least the critical limiting points of the title block and border format must be digitized or generated in the CADD system's database.

Figure 4.4 provides the recommended standard-format line offset dimensions from the cut-sheet edges for A0, A1, A2, and A3 (E, D, C, and B) sizes. The larger left-hand border space is made to accommodate bindery edge requirements for sets of drawings. The top-edge borderline condition sets a slightly larger gap than the normal edge distances to allow clearances for pin registration punching.[A11]

Because of the frequency of use of the horizontal and vertical arrangements for the A4 (A) size sheets, Figure 4.5 provides the edge-distance dimensions for each format orientation. Again, the wider left-hand edge of the vertical format and the wider top edge of the horizontal format reflect the requirements for bindery and for pin-register punching (in these two cases the offset dimensions are identical).

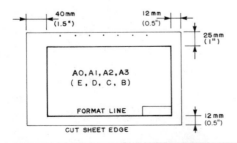

Figure 4.4 Standard large-sheet format.

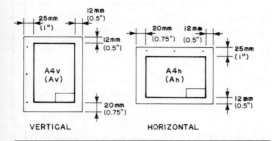

Figure 4.5 Standard small-sheet formats.

The 20-millimeter (0.75-inch) dimension shown at the bottom of the vertical format and the left-hand edge of the horizontal format reflect allowances for page-numbering systems which may be added in addition to any numbers within the drawing formats. It should be noted that this vertical and horizontal format shifting might occasionally appear for A3 (B) size sheets.

Layering conventions

The layers used in CADD systems to facilitate the handling and sharing of data now average around 1024 in number, with some systems indicating that the number of layers is practically infinite. Yet the typical CADD drawing may only require or use from 10 to 25 layers. How are these layers to be segregated for proper use?

Certain layers are set aside for standard format and housekeeping duties, and the remainder can be separated into groups as required to satisfy different disciplines or project elements. For some CADD systems, certain groups of layers could be designated as *not plotted* so as to avoid plotting such things as menu commands, timekeeping functions, or certain reference images (i.e., construction lines and digitizer input data).

For a better understanding of the transition from monolayer conventional drafting to multilayer pin graphics systems drafting to the maxilayer complexity of computer-aided design and drafting, consider the comparison shown in Figure 4.6.

The original single layer in conventional drafting, with all data readily visible, becomes a simple series of layers which must be composited to be fully viewed in pin graphics. With CADD systems, the numerous layers must be visually displayed and then readdressed and plotted to hardcopy to achieve the same result.[A12]

Even though the first layer listed in Figure 4.6 is given the number "1," this layer is often designated as layer "0" by many CADD systems. The several common and unique image layers could obviously be in-

Conventional drawing	Pin graphics composite	CADD systems display or plot
1. Single layer	Title format	Format lines
2.	Common image	Format text
3.	Description	Project titles
4.		Registration targets
5.		Grid intersects*
6.		Common-image lines
7.		Unique-image lines
8.		Common-image text
9.		Unique-image text
10.		Construction lines*
11.		Digitizer input*
12.		Review and comments*
13.		Time and data records*
14. to ?		Related discipline layers

* Layers which are normally excluded from plot file.

Figure 4.6 Comparing layering systems.

creased to accommodate specific design and drafting needs. Similarly, the common and unique text elements—such as standard title format words and notes versus project-specific titles and names—can and probably should be set onto discrete layers.

Some layers may be set aside to isolate various kinds of raw input, such as digitized data, before it is edited into the database. Also, there may be numerous additional layers assigned to disciplines that share common layers with the primary drawings.

Start layering controls by compiling a complete listing of *all available layers* and describing their normally assigned functions. Include a tabulation of the applicable logical pen and physical pen numbers and the designated display color. Refer to Figure 4.7 for a general format for this listing, and take note of the generalized breakdown of layer assignments. This first planning action will show what layer functions are available on your CADD system and can act as a checklist for each project operator.

4.2 Graphics Layering Logic: Two-Dimensional and Three-Dimensional

We live and interact in at least a four-dimensional world. Several dimensions beyond the three basic spatial directions of motion or distance and the fourth dimension—continuity of time—have even been postulated. Yet within the professional fields of design and drafting for

Layer number	Description or function	Logical pen	Physical pen	Display color
0	Unassigned data	1	—	White
99	Construction lines	1	—	Blue
100	Discipline 1, general data	1	1	White
114	Discipline 1, common image	2	2	Green
115	Discipline 1, common text	3	3	Yellow
200	Discipline 2, general data	1	1	Orange
1000	Discipline 10, general data	8	8	Red

Figure 4.7 Functional layering list (partial).

manufacturing, engineering, and architecture, conventional fabrication and construction communication is primarily a two-dimensional function which yields a two-dimensional image representing an actual three-dimensional item.

The majority of manual design and drafting utilizes a flat-surface, two-dimensional (X and Y coordinates only) medium and a marking instrument. In the CADD system, design and drafting commands initiate a database structure for lines, curves, and text, which is displayed on the terminal monitor or CRT. The visual-display function is the electromagnetic excitation of phosphors on a flat plane or series of logical planes for the CRT or monitor.[B12, B13] This CRT uses flat, two-dimensional imaging for representing three-dimensional entities.

Portrayal of three-dimensional spaces on two-dimensional surfaces requires the use of isometric projections and visual perspective approximations. The resulting two-dimensional images give an impression of depth and distance while still being communicated on a flat surface.

Communication and imaging in three dimensions requires simultaneously working in the three dimensions of space, along the X, Y, and Z axes. By manual methods this requires the building of a scale model or series of models to determine design masses and to measure fabrication

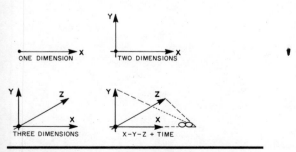

Figure 4.8 Four-dimensional interaction.

criteria. The methods for simple three-dimensional CADD imaging require describing the edges and surfaces of the objects using spatial reference points joined by straight lines and mathematically generated curves and intersects.[A3, A13]

This three-dimensional imaging is accomplished by storing the numerous coordinate points of an object for all three dimensions or axes. Three-dimensional computer-aided design and drafting allows for excellent graphic modeling of a part or assembly or complete facility by recalling to the display monitor these points and interconnects. However, the amount of memory required to store this data is very large, and the software commands are extensive. The resultant rapidly displayed images attest to the speed of the computer as it processes these myriad points of data and instructions to render a visually coherent whole. Terminal firmware may assist in manipulating these images.

Three-dimensional imaging in combination with solids modeling and FEA methods (or finite element method, FEM) greatly assists in design analysis, clearance verification, and presentations to clients. However, the subsequent communicating of a three-dimensional design with multi-angle visual displays and plotted hardcopy documents is still primarily a two-dimensional representation of the three-dimensional data. Just as with manual drafting, true three-dimensional hardcopy is sculpture—a freezing of the rhythm of design into the dynamic interplay of static elements.

Two-dimensional logic with layers

To describe a three-dimensional space using two-dimensional imaging, by either manual or CADD means, requires the drafting of at least three views 90° apart. Each view is a two-dimensional function, but the alternating side views allow for more accurate description and visual understanding.

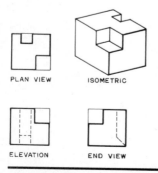

PLAN VIEW   ISOMETRIC

ELEVATION   END VIEW

Figure 4.9 Two-dimensional orthographic imaging.

Figure 4.9 delineates this three-view or *orthographic projection* method for assisting in describing an object. This method typically consists of a top view (X axis or plan view), a front view (Y axis or elevation), and at least one end view (Z axis or side elevation).[B15, B16]

To help clarify the minimally complex object shown in Figure 4.9, quite often the additional *isometric view* included here is required. This isometric, false-perspective view is accomplished by setting one or two adjacent faces at 15° (or some other selected angle) relative to the horizontal. With the edges of the object tilted or forced out of square, an apparent full view is created.

The remaining sides are projected using exact dimensions along the angled sides and vertical edges. The edge intersects of the projected lines are connected using parallel angles and 90° verticals.

Hidden surfaces

The drafting convention of hidden lines, short dashed-line segments, or lines of dots is used to render portions of objects which may not be directly visible in views of all three axes nor completely visible in the isometric. The notch in the far, top side of the object in Figure 4.9 is an example of such an image which is never completely resolved without creating another view or another isometric from a different initial point. Very complicated objects normally require many multiple views in order to avoid the confusion of numerous hidden lines.

For manufactured parts, small assemblies, whole buildings, and complete facilities, the conventional method for giving a relatively accurate two-dimensional description of a three-dimensional space is to cut selected sections and delineate the result. Figure 4.10 shows the simple, logical transition from an isometric plan view to a dotted-line representation of the complete space that is being depicted.

The angled plan view is bounded by its edges, shown in phantom lines representing the implied edge planes. Also implied by a plan (top) view is that a space usually has some finite height (or depth). This is satisfied by the phantom lines around the top edges of the space.

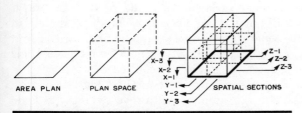

AREA PLAN   PLAN SPACE   SPATIAL SECTIONS

Figure 4.10 Two-dimensional sections through three-dimensional space.

The third view in Figure 4.10 denotes the whole space sectioned into a series of X-, Y-, and Z-axis planes. The normal convention for a plan image is that it is a horizontal section, here labeled "X-1," cut at approximately 30 centimeters (12 inches) above the horizontal surface. Subsequent horizontal sections, or lifts, are cut at various distances above the lowest surface; here labeled "X-2" and "X-3."

For depicting vertical surfaces, a similar convention is applied. The first Y-axis section, labeled "Y-1," is cut at a distance of approximately 30 centimeters (12 inches) from the farthest convenient Y plane within the space. Subsequent parallel sections at other distances are labeled "Y-2" and "Y-3."

Similarly, the Z axis can be discretely described with "Z-1," "Z-2," and "Z-3" sections at selected distances moving away from the initial Z plane. These sections are normally rigid parallel lines, representing a flat planer surface, but often they may have local offsets to capture particular data elements.

Sections X-2, Y-2, and Z-2 are further depicted with dotted lines in order to show how they would cut through a space or object and intersect one another. These intersections of planer surfaces help to depict or to capture precise points within a three-dimensional object.

Layer surfaces

Each of these sections can be also labeled as layers. Thus section X-1 would be "layer X1," section Z-2 would be "layer Z2," and so forth as required. Using conventional manual drafting methods to draw each of these layered sections would mean repeating the common section images from layer to layer.

The pin graphics systems drafting method would, on the other hand, require only the drafting of the common elements from layer X1, perhaps labeled "layer X1a," on a physically registered layer separate from the unique elements of layer X1. This second or descriptive sublayer may perhaps be logically labeled "layer X1b."

The separation of common and unique image layers of layer X1 would then allow sublayer X1a to be directly shared with layer X2, so that perhaps only the unique elements of layer X2 would need to be drawn and labeled "layer X2a." If portions of layer X2 could be shared in layer X3, then the further separation of images might be in order. And similarly, layer-sections Y1, Y2, Y3 and Z1, Z2, Z3 could have their common images separated out and shared as required.

Pin graphics, though, is a manual drafting method and even with the sharing of images, the above example could prove tedious. Its logic is, however, the precursor to CADD in that these layering methods and numbering or labeling criteria are also followed in electronic drafting.

Because of the memory capacity, rapidity, and maxinumber of available layers of the CADD system, this discrete isolation and sharing of data elements and layers is made highly productive.

Three-dimensional imaging with layers

Once the logic of manipulating intersecting spatial planes (layers or sections) is understood—and it is only really understood by actually doing it yourself—then the stage is set for considering the manipulation of finite points, planar surfaces, and solid shapes with three axes of reference.[A14, A15]

For an excellent study of the logic of three-dimensional images and two-dimensional projections of three-dimensional images, review *Fundamentals of Interactive Computer Graphics*[B13] by Foley and Van Dam. Their coverage of the subject and their diagrams are very easily interpreted and quite applicable to the concepts in this book.

Staying with the theme of this book, which is to pursue CADD as a helpful imaging-process tool-system whose ultimate output must accurately describe the object and is for the most part hardcopy, consider the wire-frame cube in Figure 4.11. If the three-dimensional CADD image were displayed and plotted using all available information and thus all lines and curves, the result might prove to be too complicated to be properly read.

View *a* in Figure 4.11 shows one face only of the tilted cubic structure shown in the remaining views; actually this face could be considered as a precisely lined-up version of view *b,* with the lines of the other planes actually being drawn on top of one another. The image in view *b* depicts all edges of the cube with solid lines; the appearance is that of a framework of wires, hence "wire frame."

The ambiguity of this wire-frame display is that the viewing angle of the cube could be construed as that of the surface shown either in view *c* or in view *d.* That layers and dotted or hidden lines are useful tools in this endeavor is shown by the clearly defined display of view *e.*

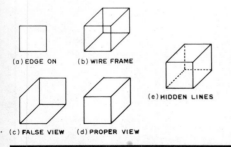

(a) EDGE ON   (b) WIRE FRAME

(e) HIDDEN LINES

(c) FALSE VIEW   (d) PROPER VIEW

Figure 4.11 Wire-frame ambiguity.

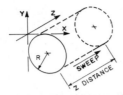

Figure 4.12 Creating a simple CADD solid.

Consider the circle in view *a* of Figure 4.12 as a flat circular plane, made of individually definable points, which has the thickness of a point. All the points on this circular plane can be described with differing combinations of X- and Y-axis numbers, but with only one Z-axis reference number—it is a circular plane that is one point thick.

To create a reference solid shape, for example the cylinder shown, the circular plane of points can be swept through a finite distance along the Z axis. Thus the "solid" cylindrical shape shown can be defined by a set number of points, each with specific X-, Y-, and Z-axis reference numbers. Similarly, rectangular, square, triangular, and regular polygon shapes can be manipulated, and then described, as solid sets of points in space.

Boolean geometry

These simple "solid" shapes, or primitives, can be combined to make any number of complex shapes using Boolean geometry. This method of controlling the individual points of these "solid" shapes is a symbolic algebraic logic process first developed by George Boole, circa 1847.[B1] The probability of these points' moving and combining as mathematically described sets allows the development of CADD software for solids modeling.

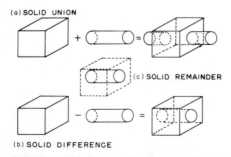

Figure 4.13 Boolean transformations.

The simple cube and cylinder of Figure 4.13 can be combined by *addition (union)* or *subtraction (difference)* to form the cube with handles in view *a* or the cube with a hole through it in view *b*. A third state is also available, the *remainder (intersection)*, as shown in view *c*. This third state could be construed as the filled hole of view *b*. Further manipulation of these shapes includes treating them as surfaces rather than solids and the finite "tweaking" of individual elements.[A3, A13, A14, A15]

Typically, three-dimensional CADD software systems display a calculated three-dimensional image, from a selected viewing angle, as a series of points and lines in one of these forms:

- *Wire frame.*   All lines and edges are shown.
- *Hidden lines dotted.*   Lines and edges not directly seen from the viewing angle are displayed as a dotted- or dashed-line series.
- *Hidden lines removed.*   Lines and edges not directly seen from the viewing angle are not displayed.

On some CADD systems, these hidden lines, representing the edges not in view, are generated as a set of calculated points and dotted or dashed lines on a separate layer. By manipulating the layer commands either to "turn off" (not to display) or to "turn on" (to display) the layer with the hidden lines, the display image can be changed back and forth between view *d* and view *e* in Figure 4.11.

Depending upon the individual three-dimensional CADD software, object layout and construction lines may be on separate layers from the data elements and command functions which are required to generate the three-dimensional image. Further, previously generated three-dimensional images may be placed on an inactive, or unhittable, layer so that other design elements may be generated in three dimensions on the same sheet for comparisons.

4.3 Graphics Layering Logic: Solids Modeling

Although it is not the province of this book to describe in depth the workings of CADD software systems, some discussion of solids modeling is in order. A solid object, or a real-life object, can be depicted with a close measure of accuracy on CADD systems by using three-dimensional image handling plus a series of logical steps to handle the finite elements that describe combinations of primitive geometric structures. Rather than working with just surface modeling, connecting the edges of the wire frames to form planes, let us dwell upon the use of three-dimensional solid geometry, which is far more useful for spatial design and drafting.

Solid designs

The value of solids-modeling exercises is in the combinations of masses and shapes that are the essence of project design. These solid forms are not just surfaces or wire frames as in standard three-dimensional work, but rather fully defined spaces that can be used to determine the interaction of volumes. A solid set of points can easily be checked for coincidence with another set of points, which not only would indicate that one object has "hit" another but also would show the depth and breadth of the penetration.

Fully utilized three-dimensional solids modeling rivals the creation of physical models, molds, and sculptures for the determination of construction tolerances and arrangements. With sequential addition of CADD solids, by critical path methodology, an erection clearance and sequence mode can be determined and checked without the normal hassles of physical models and endless erection sketches.[A16]

Three-dimensional solids modeling is also the basis for numerical control of manufacturing tool paths and robotic movements.[A17] A dynamically controlled solid shape, or a tool, can be directed to intersect a (rotating) solid shape, or to forge it, and the resultant differential in material removed can then be counted and reclaimed for recycling.

After the three-dimensional solids modeling has accomplished its design (clearances) task, and the visual display or displays are approved, the hardcopy output must be generated. The complex nature of the three-dimensional solid is not viewed or felt in its solid form (sets of points) but rather as visible surfaces. These surfaces can be captured in photographs or two-dimensional plots. But the hardcopy plots will only delineate the edges of the surfaces, or the facet lines of the FEA description (which is the same thing).

Thus, most hardcopy output is a two-dimensional representation of the three-dimensional solid. Only the sculptural form, possibly made by robotics, is the true three-dimensional image.

4.4   Graphics Layering Logic: Color

Why color? Color communicates! The trend is toward an information-based society, handling and interacting with massive amounts of information and data. Reception of this ever-increasing amount of data must be at a rate that is compatible with the most efficient method of input; larger amounts of information can be discerned (by humans) when it is presented in layers of color than when it appears as all black on white.[A18]

Compare the data communication capabilities of a multidiscipline image rendered in high-contrast black and white (or blue on white) with the same image that has the common background data screen-tinted or subdued to light gray (or light blue) relative to a specific discipline in full tone. Compare selected areas in Figure 4.14 with the corresponding portions of Figure 4.15. Note that portions of the images have been screen-tint-subdued to 30 percent of their full-solid value in Figure 4.15. The black over grey of the partially screened image demonstrates how much better even monochromatic color tinting communicates than does an all-full-tone, high-contrast image.[B7]

Similarly, but on a much greater data-handling scale, multilayers of data presented in multicolors communicate better than monochrome. Compare a CADD plot using separate colors for each discipline-layer with a similar monochromatic plot: Which appears to communicate the desired information with better clarity?

The bottom line is that the expense of color monitors, software support, and plotters is coming down for CADD installations. And the demand is up for data represented or displayed in colors. But color is a two-edged sword. While color communicates better, it requires even greater design and drafting output planning.[A19]

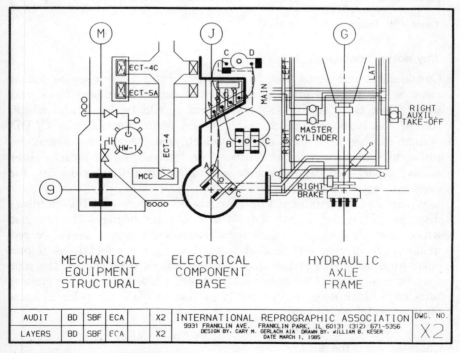

Figure 4.14 Standard full tone imagery.

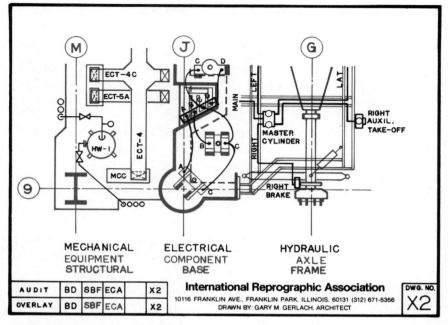

		MECHANICAL EQUIPMENT STRUCTURAL		ELECTRICAL COMPONENT BASE		HYDRAULIC AXLE FRAME		
AUDIT	BD	SBF	ECA		X2	**International Reprographic Association** 10116 FRANKLIN AVE., FRANKLIN PARK, ILLINOIS, 60131 (312) 671-5356 DRAWN BY: GARY M. GERLACH, ARCHITECT	DWG. NO. X2	
OVERLAY	BD	SBF	ECA		X2			

Figure 4.15 Image with partial tinting.

Why not monochrome?

Consider the end result first: Is the current project hardcopy output in color or black and white? If it is in the current standard black and white, then the CADD hardcopy output should be black and white. And if the hardcopy output is black and white, possibly the CADD system display need only be in monochrome. Monochrome may be sufficient, with certain layers "current" or "active" and set for a brighter display aspect and the remainder set "off" with a dimmer display, for even interactive checking.

Where CADD systems utilize monochromatic screen (CRT-monitor) displays, be reminded that today's monochrome displays are not just white lines on a black field. Some displays have amber, green, or red imagery on varying screen field tints. The overall effect is as if one color were displayed, rather than multiple colors, even though the plot may be multicolor. Also note that standard white (or green or amber) lines on a black field are eventually plotted as black (or colored) lines on a typically white field.

Choosing color for display

Unfortunately, most CADD systems use display monitors with a black field for the images and colors. The current ergonomics and power loadings of monitor displays typically do not provide for comfortable displaying of black or colored lines on a white field. Yet most color hardcopy output utilizes a white field.

Perhaps it would be possible to begin the discussion of color by seeking a compromise: an 18 percent gray monitor background provides a much livelier field on which to display color. A very dynamic reference of this condition can be viewed in Barbara Meier's article, "BUCOLIC: A Program for Teaching Color Theory to Art Students."[A20] Although her discussion covers very precise relationships between hue, saturation, and value, the overall presentation method may serve to ease some CADD display functions.

Figure 4.16 provides a correlation of the standard four-color process colors (magenta, yellow, cyan, and black), the seven full-typical (primary) colors and several secondary (lighter) colors, plus the classic black and white "colors." Rather than merely color names, this chart also provides a preliminary cross reference to the Pantone Matching System (PMS) color formula guide numbers. These are one of the standard sources for colors used in offset printing. Please see a color chart for full-color reference. (The PMS numbers given here are for coated stock, subscript c; numbers for uncoated stock are similar, subscript u, but the hue and tint of the final image will be somewhat different.[A21])

COLOR NAMES		Standard Pantone PMS numbers (coated stock)	DISPLAY SYSTEMS	
Process image	Typical image		Display color	Logical pen
Black	Black	Process black	White*	1
White	White	Process white	Black	—
Magenta	Red	032c	Red	2
Yellow	Yellow	Process yellow	Yellow	5†
Cyan	Blue	Process blue	Blue	4
Three-color	Brown	195c	Sepia	7†
	Green	354c	Green	3
	Orange	021c	Orange	6†
	Purple	265c	Purple	8†
	30% gray	428c	Light gray	5†
	50% gray	430c	Dark gray	
	Pink	210c	Light red	6†
	Tan	155c	Light brown	
	Light green	351c	Light green	7†
	Dark blue	Reflex blue	Dark blue	
	Light blue	292c	Light blue	8†

* White: may be amber or red in some monochrome systems
† May not match with physical pen.

Figure 4.16 Color standards for CADD display.

It should be noted at the outset that the color intensities, saturations, and values displayed on the CADD monitor are a function of the CRT video-imaging devices. The red-green-blue (RGB) light sources are used additively (the full combination gives white) to produce the observed colors. The vector-plotted, hardcopy colors, on the other hand, are subtractive combinations (full mixing produces brown-black, similar to the three-color process image) of opaque and semiopaque pigments.[A22, A39, A40]

The magenta, yellow, cyan, and black process colors named in this figure are currently matched by the rasterized output devices such as color electrostatic plotters, color laser printers, and color ink-jet systems. Thus, certain aspects of these suggested display color standards are already in place. And in some cases, they are utilized by CADD system vendors. Refer to *Inside AutoCAD* by Dan Raker and H. Rice.[B14]

Developing standards

Figure 4.16 provides color references that can be a starting point for the development of standard CADD displays, matching plotter imaging, and subsequent truer reproduction of designer-drafter selected colors. Swatch cards with these colors can be used to visually integrate the several systems.

With these basic, standard colors (or with subsequent reference number modifications as determined) built into the CADD software and supported by display systems manufacturers and plotter pen manufacturers, hardcopy output imaging and monitor display imaging can be relatively closely matched by using PMS color swatches.

The intent is to have the first four or seven basic colors of all systems initially match a common standard. Specialty hues and tints could then be easily established or mixed as alternatives when required by specific system operators.

4.5   Operator-Machine Interface

Expanding upon John Naisbitt's theme, "high tech/high touch," in *Megatrends,*[B17] consider for a moment just how the designer or drafter communicates with a CADD system.

The first point of interface is *touching the keyboard.* Just as it is true that a CADD system operator does not need to know how to program software but merely how to use it, so also the operator of a CADD system keyboard does not need to know how to type 150 words per minute but needs merely to be acquainted with the approximate locations of the keys and what they represent.

The next items that must be touched in order to use the electronic drafting machine are the *joystick* or the *thumb wheels* used to control the cursor position. The joystick can be used by either the right or left hand to drive the active reference point to the intended location, with better control than up-down-right-left arrow keys. Thumb wheels, on the other hand, may not be as easily operated and usually are not located conveniently for left-handed people. A close alternative to these functions is the *roller ball* or *track ball,* which may be found to provide excellent cursor control.

These input functions might also be handled by using a *probe pen* or *mouse or puck* digitizer input device. Moving on a surface separate from the keyboard, these devices usually include several function keys to allow preset direct commands to be entered at given positions.

Some CADD workstations include the sophisticated hardware necessary to support commands input and cursor control by actually touching the monitor screen. Using a light-source pen, a digitizer–probe pen, or simply a finger can initiate functions by engaging light-sensitive or electromagnetic grids which are coupled with the CRT surface.

Possibly the lightest touches of all for commands input are used with the latest systems, which include *voice recognition.* They are so high-tech as to need no physical touch.

Getting your directions in

The design or layout of the keyboard, and the understanding of its use, is the first hurdle to be cleared in operating the electronic drafting tool. Set aside, for later use, the manual drafting implements of the track-drafting machine, parallel bar, adjustable triangle, and pens and pencils. Design and drafting with CADD requires the learning of alphanumeric command sequences and the positioning of a *cursor* as an electronic reference point for imaging by initiating those preset commands.

With input via the keyboard and cursor control devices, output response back to the operator is from the monitor CRT. In order to make the input commands somewhat easier, these cursor control devices are often coupled with a *commands menu,* or selection format. The commands menu can be displayed on the CRT monitor or printed onto the surface of a separate digitizer board.

Commands menus provide shorthand designations and symbolic icons for preset strings of often-used instructions. Rather than tediously typing in the necessary command-sequence alphabetical and numeric characters, you can access them by initiating a probe on the zone of the menu image. To be truly productive, these CADD menu commands must be revisable by the (key) system operator, and it must be possible to create and insert into the software structure additional menu commands, or macros, with suitable icon symbols.

Communicating

In manual drafting, physical drafting tools are used in a systematic manner to communicate a design via hardcopy. With CADD systems, the physical electronic drafting tools that we touch are decidedly different from T squares, triangles, and pens, but the logic of image creation is much the same.

The design or drafting operator of a CADD system must call up or access a predetermined, formatted sheet from the file, select the proper logical pen with at least a certain color attribute, and then draw by generating graphic elements of given line sizes and types, as well as text elements of given font style and height. The lines, curves, and text will be on several preselected layers and the database must be filed.

Simple test procedure

Follow the specific steps in the simplified test procedure below to verify whether the training programs, special assistance, and personal reading of the operator's manual have accomplished their task. Is your operator-to-machine interface an easy and confident communication process? Can you step through each CADdrafting procedure in preparation for doing the CADesign work that is necessary?

1. On a selected layer, with a selected logical pen, initiate a starting point and generate a selected line type in color for a distance of 50 millimeters (1.995 inches) at an up angle of 60° from the horizontal. Continue this first line, or initiate a second line, from the second or previous end point for a horizontal distance of 50 millimeters (1.995 inches). Continue with a line from the last point at a down angle of 60° for again 50 millimeters (1.995 inches).

Complete the hexagon image. End the line and file this drawing with the label and date "TEST:mm/dd/yy." Clear the screen and then recall the filed drawing.

2. Touch, access, grab, or group the hexagon-shaped line sequence, copy the set, and place a copy of the image on another layer. Change the color of the copied hexagonal shape. Access an edge point of the hexagonal shape on one layer, move the shape, and set the chosen point *coincident* with a similar point on the original hexagon (which is on another layer). Rotate the second hexagon so that two points, one line edge, are coincident. Zoom in to verify coincidence, and display comparative X and Y coordinates to ascertain precision.

Repeat this step as required to verify procedures.

3. On a third layer, draw a different line type with a different logical pen in a different color with a different line thickness between any two

distant points on the two, now coincident, hexagonal shapes. Verify the precision of point capture. Repeat this process at or from midpoints of certain facet edges. Create a line segment perpendicular to a facet edge. Create a circular line element tangent to a facet edge.

File this drawing as "revision 1" to the previous "TEST:mm/dd/yy" drawing, without revising the original.

4. On a fourth layer, initiate a text element or series with a different logical pen in a different color, and label each shape. Rotate, move, copy, and rescale the text images to test each function.

File this as "revision 2" to the previous sets. Clear the screen and recall "revision 2 of TEST:mm/dd/yy." Clear the screen and recall the original drawing, "TEST:mm/dd/yy."

5. Incorporate a title block and border format layer or layers, and create a plot file for "revision 2 of TEST:mm/dd/yy." Set up the plotter and plot the drawing. Scale the plot to verify accuracy of line images, coincident points, and command over colors, layers, and text fonts.

6. Return to the "revision 2 of TEST:mm/dd/yy" file and modify whatever needs to be done. Refile as "revision 3 of TEST:mm/dd/yy." Reconfigure a plot file and plot again.

7. (Optional) For systems with three-dimensional capability: following the procedure outlined in steps 1 and 2, create a 5-sided figure, a pentagon. Copy this figure and then attach it to each of the five sides. By folding the edges and then continuing to replicate the pentagon, the operator should be able to create a 32-sided, wire-frame hollow polyhedron. The spherical image thus created is a simulation of the molecule C_{60}, which three-dimensional shape has been fondly named "Buckminsterfullerene."[A47] If the operator is successful, your CADD system can handle such structures as geodesic domes.

With these basics out of the way, you can now proceed to do in-fill patterns, sectionings, symbols, autodimensioning, etc., with the remainder of your CADD system's capabilities. You are on your own! And it can be lonely unless you have a good operator's manual, a competent support service, or a consultant.

Chapter

5

Hardcopy Output Managing

After putting an extensive amount of system hardware, program software, work-hours (wetware), training, raw data information, and money into your new CADD system, what did you get in return? If you invested the same dollars, no, just 10 or 30 percent of the CADD system dollars, in a designer, an engineer, a part-time drafter, or even a clerk, what output should you expect? What form of test would be suitable for testing the production capability of your newly hired machine or human staff?

Figure 5.1 provides a basic answer to these questions. The output from the professional must be suitable to the next user, the client, so

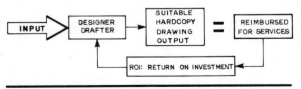

Figure 5.1 Input, then output, then ROI.

that a direct return on invested time, energy, and dollars can be realized. Refer to Figure 1.6 for a direct step-through of the procedures leading from input to the designer-operator who uses the appropriate tools for proper quality output.

Conventionally, production output is reviewed on the basis of the number of hours per finished drawing. The prints from the completed drawings then can be shown to the client to prove professional services were rendered so as to receive a return on your investment. Average costs per drawing were considered in Chapter 2 and derive from direct responses to the items in Figures 2.1 through 2.4.

With CADD, the production output is basically in three forms:

1. Visual two-dimensional display of the three-dimensional database

2. Electromagnetic softcopy to disk or tape

3. Plotted, printed, or projected hardcopy on film, paper, metal, or plastic

The first output form may produce ROI from the client if all that is necessary is a visual demonstration of service. Electromagnetic soft-copy should produce ROI provided that the client company wants input to its computer system as a volatile database. Typically, the useful forms of production output from CADD are the numerous hardcopy medias.

The final form of the plotted output from CADD may have a significant impact on system selection and use. The logical points below were posed in Chapter 4, Section 4.4, in the discussion of setting up a CADD system for color. The points are listed again here to reinforce the concept that *the next use of any* (hardcopy) *image* must be considered before the creation of that image.

1. Is the current project hardcopy output in color or black and white?

2. If the output is in the standard black and white, then the CADD hardcopy output probably should be black and white.

3. If the output is black and white, possibly the CADD system display need only be in monochrome.

4. If the CADD system display is polychrome for enhanced communication, then probably the hardcopy output should be multicolor in order to communicate at a similar level.

It is well known that the information-handling capabilities of color differentiation may be very valuable and necessary for CADesign and CADrafting and in checking CADD output. Should, then, the plotted output be consistent in information-handling capability and therefore be in color, or need it only revert back to the traditional black and white? A monochrome plot image derived from color display will require extra planning to create the extra layers and drawings.

5.1 Input from the Output Standpoint

If ink-on-film drafting creates the fastest, densest image and is the best archival drafting medium, why would anyone hire a drafter who works only with ballpoint or felt-tip pen on bond or vellum? Just because this drafter is faster at making revisions?[A23]

Happily, CADD is not just a drafter; it is also a design assistant. Were the CADD system only a CADrafting system, the ambiguity of using the system to its best advantage might be more easily resolved. When all is said and done, the CADD system in its electromagnetic functioning and display mode becomes a production drafting tool for rapidly plotting "offline originals."

Is this rapid electronic drafter working according to your office standards? Are your presentation packages enhanced by its hardcopy output? Are the plotted contract construction and fabrication documents suitable for the typical reprographic procedures that your project requires?[A23] The answer to each of these questions can and should be "yes."

In the healthy transition to CADD, the move from conventional drafting to pin graphics overlay drafting to CADD's electronic layer drafting can be quite smooth if the logical planning steps are included. Figure 4.1 in Chapter 4 delineates the logical continuity of these output trails. Figure 5.2 lists some of the drafting functions that are normally accomplished for all three systems.

The process of drafting produces hardcopy which is either intended for display or specifically used as a vehicle for further reproductions. CADD ranks very high in the comparisons in Figure 5.2. However, the functions listed must be anticipated and programmed into the software in order to achieve proper performance from the hardware.

The bottom line in this figure shows a value added of 2:1 (above the value of conventional drafting) for systems-overlay drafting; this value added is attributed primarily to sharing of data, which makes in unnecessary to draw or revise the same line twice. This increase is accomplished with the same staff but may require investment in a $15 pinbar. In addition, a possible doubling of reproduction costs (from 1.2 to 2.0 percent of fees) may be expected. Yet this 2:1 increase in productivity with very little increase in expenses could mean approximately a 50 percent increase in profitability.[A1]

Accomplishing the same tasks as conventional and systems drafting, only doing it much faster, is the province of CADD. The anticipated 4:1 productivity increase ratio is achieved only at the level of a minimum $20,000 investment in hardware, software, and training. Initial pro-

Drafting function	Conventional Drafting	Pin graphic systems	CADD
Sketching	Yes	Layers	Layers
Erasure	Yes	Yes	Instantly
Graphite lead	Yes	Yes	Some
Plastic lead	Yes	Yes	No
Electrostatics	Rare	Good	Fastest
Ballpoint pen	Poor	Poor	Very fast
Felt-tip pen	Yes	Yes	Fast
Liquid-ink pen	Best	Best	Slowest
Taping	Yes	Yes	Line types
Stamps	Yes	Yes	Symbols
Stick-ons	Yes	Yes	Symbols
Colors	Some	Yes	Preferred
Cut and tape	Rare	Yes	Instantly
Photodrafting	Rare	Excellent	Rare
Overlays	No	Registered	Layers
Micrographics	Yes	Yes	COM
Filing	Flat	Vertical	Recallable
AVERAGE COSTS:			
Personnel	$ base	$ base	$ + $5000
Equipment	On hand	$15 pinbar	$30,000 min.
Supplies	Same	2:1 in film	10:1 to 20:1
Reproduction	Same	Double	Double +
Total added	Even	$15 + repro	$40K + repro
Value added	Nil	2:1 output	2:1, 4:1, or better output

Figure 5.2 Drafting functions by system.

ductivity with CADD, for those drawings on which it is used, just barely approaches 1:1. However, experienced drafter-operators can achieve well over the 4:1 ratio using established databases.

One often overlooked and very interesting aspect of computer-aided design and drafting is that the continual replotting of the entire original can chew up 10 to 20 times as much drafting paper, vellum, or film as would be used by manual methods. Each time the drawing is replotted, the old plot copy is thrown away (or worse yet, it is filed!)[A1]

It is precisely the CADD plotter's speed which allows each previous "hardcopy original" to be wasted. This use of material is similar to that of a manual drafter who *throws the drawing away and starts over from scratch* after each mistake or simple revision.[A24] See Chapter 7 for discussions on repligraphic drafting alternatives to these functions.

Input for graphic lines output

To draw with CADD means to enter a series of commands which cause a database to be generated; the database can be displayed as an image on the monitor with several layers and logic pens and colors; the image can later be plotted as hardcopy. This series of moves is similar to picking up a technical drafting pen, of a set line-width size and predetermined ink color, then proceeding to illustrate graphic lines and text.

Building upon Figure 4.7, the physical pen in the plotter should correspond to the logical pen in the software system. Further, the line thickness designated by the physical pen should be matched by the CADD display image of line thickness.

In manual drafting, based upon traditions of drafting procedures, certain elements of a drawing are consistently rendered with varying line widths in order to fully communicate the design. These standards for drafting are a part of every professional design and drafting firm *and need to apply also to the CADD, the rapid electronic drafter.* Refer to *Recommended Standards for Production Procedures,*[B11] by the Committee on Production Office Procedures (POP) of the Northern California Chapter of the American Institute of Architects, edited by August Strotz.

Modern drafting techniques indicate that the standard differentiation of line types by means of line thickness is fully compatible with the requirements of computer-assisted drafting. In fact, the varying line thicknesses are already handled in a standard fashion by the technical pen manufacturers.[A21, A25]

Figure 5.3 tabulates a suggested use of the standard plotter pen sizes matched to the software logical pen functions in the CADD systems. The "standards" suggestion here is that the displayed lines assigned to

| Software logical pen | Plotter physical pen | STANDARD | | | | Display or plot color |
| | | Line thickness | | | Display rasters | |
		Pen No.	Millimeters	Inch		
1	1	00	0.30	0.012	1	Black and white
2	2	0	0.35†	0.014	1	Red
3	3	2	0.60	0.024	2	Green
4	4*	2½	0.70†	0.028	2	Blue
5	5*	1	0.50	0.020	2	Yellow
6	6*	3	0.80	0.031	2	Orange
7	7*	3½	1.00	0.039	4	Brown
8	8*	4	1.20	0.047	4	Purple

* May not have a matching logical pen.
† ISO and ANSI standards for thin and thick lines.

Figure 5.3 Standards for physical and logical pens.

logical pen 1 should have a similar line thickness or display aspect to that of the matching physical pen. For example, the lines (and text) displayed by logical pen 3 could be twice as thick or bold as those displayed by logical pen 1 in order to match the plotted image of their corresponding physical pens. This figure provides corresponding physical line thickness and approximations regarding display resolution.[A21, A26]

The majority of vector plotters currently in use have penholders for from one to four pens. Some plotter systems allow upward of eight physical pens at any time. Unfortunately, not all the CADD software systems can designate eight logical pens; many systems max-out at three logical pens. Some of this problem is compensated for by assigning specific layers to selected physical pens: all lines and text on a layer are assigned to a specific physical pen for line weight (and color).

Figure 5.3 does not attempt to show all the pen combinations that could occur beyond a typical set of four, except to list a possible next set of four. Although pen sizes smaller than 00 are marketed, their very small diameters often cannot stand up to extended high-volume plotting. Likewise, although pen sizes run up through number 14, with a 6.00-millimeter (0.236-inch) line width, the typical maximum technical pen plotter point is number 4, 1.20 millimeters (0.047 inch).[A25]

The standards in Figure 5.3 are all satisfactory for technical, liquid-ink plotter pens and would allow easy adaptation for later matching of manual drafting if required on the hardcopy plots. However, ballpoint and felt-tip plotter pens do not have corresponding penpoint (and thus line width) controls. In some cases, ballpoints intended are designated as thin or wide, depending primarily on intended medium type. No real attempt has yet to be made to configure ballpoints and felt tips to true line-width controls.

Using the suggested line resolution (display raster) column, the software logic required to display varying line thicknesses (by parallel repainting), image intensity variations, and field fills, might be easily added to the user's workstation configuration. These multiple-stroke concepts might also be adapted to driving the vector plotter ballpoints and felt tips in a similar fashion to achieve comparable final image control over line thickness.

These same software requirements for displayed line-thickness differentiation would also be configured to handle the output requirements for the raster-imaging techniques of electrostatic and ink-jet plotters. Photoplotters handle this problem with variable aperture controls, dwell time, and light intensity.

From color to black and white

Where CADD systems utilize monochromatic monitor screen displays but expect to plot in color, or where color monitor images will not be reflected in the plotted output, there may be a coordination problem in converting from color to black and white. This translation can be achieved with designated line forms that correlate a specific color to a particular graphic representation of a line.

Figure 5.4 captures the pertinent display color standards information from Figure 4.16 and adds a black-and-white field-fill adaptation. These graphic alternatives to color are based upon the standard, ancient heraldic graphic representations for colors. The reference here is to page 77 of the excellent book *Color,*[B18] edited by Helen Varley.

Compare the CADD display image colors listed in Figure 5.4 with the anticipated hardcopy plot color names. Next is a cross-reference sequence for physical pens that may match logical pens and colors within the CADD software. The right-hand column offers the linear graphic, black and white, representations for matching monochrome field-fill plots with the original displayed colors.

If the CADD system displays only in monochrome, these linear graphic representations can be the displayed field fills which will eventually be plotted in colors. The width and separation of the displayed lines should be correlated with plotter output to achieve uniform filling, with line overlap, of the designated fields.[A21]

STANDARD DISPLAY COLOR			RELATED PLOT GRAPHICS		
Display image	Pantone PMS numbers (coated stock)		Plot color	Physical pen	Black and white field fill
Black	Process black		—	—	▓
White*	Process white		Black	1	▢
Magenta	032c		Red	2	
Yellow	Process yellow		Yellow	5‡	
Cyan	Process blue		Blue	4†	
Brown	195c		Sepia	7‡	
Green	354c		Green	3	
Orange	021c		Orange	6‡	
Purple	265c		Purple	8‡	
30% gray	428c		Light gray	5‡	
50% gray	430c		Dark gray		
Pink	210c		Light red	6‡	
Tan	155c		Light brown		
Light green	351c		Light green	7‡	
Dark blue	Reflex blue		Dark blue		
Light blue	292c		Light blue	8‡	

* White; may be amber or red in some monochrome systems.
† Blue may fade out during further reproductions.
‡ May not match with logical pen; see Figure 4.16.

Figure 5.4 Black-and-white field fills from color.

Exceptions (by this author) to the referenced source[B18] are:

1. "White" is a solid fill.
2. "50% gray" is a dashed-line mesh.
3. "Black" is a solid-line mesh.
4. "30% gray" is a dotted-line mesh.
5. "Dark (reflex) blue" is solid horizontal lines.
6. "Medium (process) blue" is dashed horizontal lines.
7. "Light blue" is dotted horizontal lines.
8. "Brown" is vertical wavy solid lines.
9. "Tan" is vertical wavy dashed lines.
10. "Orange" is vertical zigzag lines.
11. "Light green" is dashed up-to-left 45° lines.
12. "Pink" (light red) is dashed vertical lines

Input for consistent text output

Just as drafted lines have standard widths or thicknesses, so too there are current standards for text heights and font styles which are not being fully addressed by all CADD systems vendors. Figure 5.5 provides a preliminary listing of text sizes from a very minimum 10 point [International Organization for Standardization (ISO) minimum of 2.5 millimeters (0.100 inch)], through the suggested American National Standards Institute (ANSI) micrographics minimum of 12 point [3.5 millimeters (0.125 inch)] to the normal maximum text size of 36 point [10.0 millimeters (0.375 inch)].[B19, B20, B21]

STANDARD TEXT HEIGHTS				RECOMMENDED PLOTTER PENS			
Typesetting point	Lettering guide	Inch	Millimeter	Minimum pen	Maximum pen	Standard pen	Logical pen
10	100	0.100	2.50*	00	1	00	1
12	120	0.125*	3.50	00	2	0	1
18	175	0.175	5.00	0	3	1	2
24	240	0.250	7.00	1	4†	2½	3
36	350	0.350	10.00	2	4†	3	4

† Maximum plotter point may be size 4.
* ISO (millimeter) and ANSI (inch) standards for minimum letter height.

Figure 5.5 Standards for text sizes.

Figure 5.5 also covers the suggested matching standard manual lettering guides and the recommended plotter pens to suit the particular size of text. The ranges of pen sizes are given, based upon lettering-guide recommendations; however, the standard pen figure should give the best results by not being too thin a line and by also avoiding plugging the centers of closed letters with lines that are too fat.[A21]

Particular text font styles become subjective very fast, and in some cases they are trademark-restricted. However, adoption of certain basic styles to match existing lettering guides would be generally beneficial. Text fonts and styles must also match individual office standards as well as the suggested international (ISO) and American (ANSI) standards.[B19, B20, B21]

Of particular importance is *slant:* most AEC and manufacturing design lettering is straight up and down, vertical, while many standard CADD systems plot text at a slant even though the displayed text image is vertical. Consistent use of vertical text is required as the initial standard.

Each of these line and text specifications should be incorporated into your CADD system software. In most cases, these workstation configurations can be modified, and special prompting and support macros can be created to augment implementation.

5.2   Output Devices and Functions

Once the CADD system has been configured to accomplish productive and integrated electronic drafting, then the output functions take on new meaning. At this point the specific type of CADD interactive graphic system is not of primary concern. Nor are we involved directly with output to a display monitor. And softcopy or electromagnetic output is still a separate matter. It now is time to review the several types of hardcopy that can be obtained from a (generic) CADD system.

Looking primarily at this hardcopy condition, Figure 5.6 attempts to construct the typical logic tree for some of the numerous alternate hardcopy forms available.[A27, S1, S2, S3] Several decisions are required in order to select the proper hardcopy type to match the corresponding positions in the design process. Refer to Figures 3.4 and 3.7 for diagrams of the standard linear flow of the design process and hardcopy considerations.

Keeping to the drafting-hardcopy output theme, consider Figure 5.6 first from the graphics pen-plotter standpoint alone. As amply discussed below in this section, the plotting or printing medium for each form of output must be suitable for the final surface on which the image will appear. Hardcopy output from an alphanumeric printer is to be considered separately (see Figure 1.19), since it cannot create the graphics output required for CADD imaging.

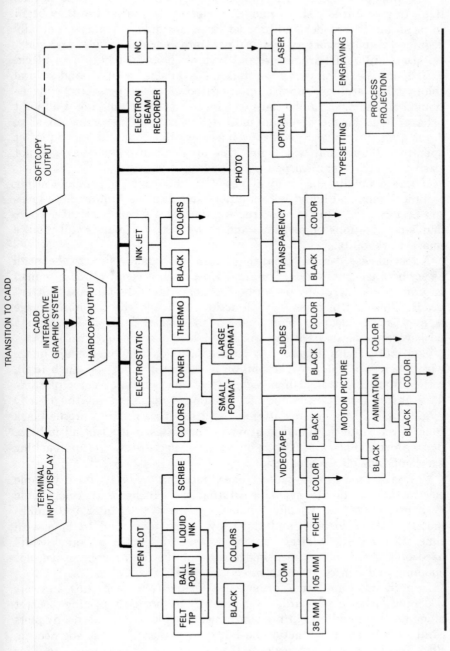

Figure 5.6 Hardcopy decision tree.

The first pen-plot form shown is the felt-tip variety. These fibrous tips can give initially sharp images. Unfortunately, after use they begin to mush out to broader and broader lines, and image quality eventually degrades to unsatisfactory. Felt-tip pens are available in fine- and wide-tip sizes, different hardnesses, and several colors in addition to black.

Ballpoint pens for vector plotters are available in black and several colors. They are configured as pressurized cartridge pens, the conventional ballpoints, and roller balls which use a freer-flowing ink. Ballpoint pens provide longer life than most felt tips, but they start to skip, developing intermittent voids in ink flow, too soon for most plotter operators. Thin- and wide-point tips are available, but they are not sized to match technical pen-point widths.

If image quality for archival needs is important, a pen plot using technical pens and liquid ink on a polyester drafting film medium gives the best results. This is also true for the cases when later off-system, hands-on additions or revisions and reproduction demands will require image workability.

A special-case, "scribe" condition is also shown here. Numerical control of scribe angle, draw direction, and tip pressure could produce a map base of similar hardcopy on scribe-coat material with standard "cutter" heads. This is still a pen-type function, although the resultant image is a negative (clear or light line on an opaque field) rather than a positive (opaque or dark line on a translucent or opaque field).

Continuing with Figure 5.6, electrostatic plotters create an image with a series of dots, at a resolution of 200 to 400 dots per inch (dpi), rather than the straight-line segments of the pen-type vector plotters. This raster format is similar to the image displayed on the CADD monitor CRT. An electrostatic plot typically uses a monochrome black toner on a white field, and it provides the fastest output of all full-size plotter forms. The current state of the art of electrostatics is approaching excellent full-color reproductions.

Primarily used as a graphite "toner" medium for better quality, some electrostatic plots are available in the less expensive thermographic systems. These are usually smaller in format, 215.90x279.40 millimeters (8½x11 inches), and the copy image may tend to fade with time. Electrostatic plotters are often used to obtain a "quick-look" hardcopy of a display screen image without the need for extensive plot spooling and pen or medium selections. (Refer to Figure 1.20.)

In both small and large formats, ink-jet plotters are finding an ever-widening niche in the hardcopy market.[A28] By precisely placing discreet amounts of colored inks at predetermined pixel locations, hardcopy plots can be produced that function both as line drawings and as engineering FEA and FEM analysis readouts (i.e., color-variations-equals-stress for structural integrities, color-equals-geology for geophysical layering, and color-equals-quantities for temperature and pressure differentials analysis).

Skip over photoplotted hardcopy for the moment and consider electron beam recording (EBR). This is a state-of-the-art hardcopy plotting function akin to photoplots and laser plots but with the "writing" head controlling a stream of electrons similar to that of television. Electron-sensitive silver-halide film emulsion is exposed by a controlled beam of electrons. CADD-generated images can be vector- or raster-plotted by EBR in a convenient, small format with a positive or negative image. Final size enlargement is usually by photoprojection with a process camera.

The next output route in Figure 5.6 is from CADD to hardcopy to NC, or alternatively from CADD to softcopy to NC. This reflects the digital control of X, Y, and Z axes by numerical control and robotics devices which ultimately produce some form of hardcopy. It should be noted that the realm of NC is a special case.[A17] All other hardcopy methods (except for advanced laser holography, which is really not "hard" at all) produce two-dimensional images; you cannot truly draw three dimensions on a flat surface.

Only through NC and its related cousins can actual "drawings" of the three-dimensional images from CADesign and CADD be created by *sculpting* the image. Hence, although the main line of NC is thought of as via the hardcopy channel, the software de-spooling procedure does not cause a pen to draw but rather, using electromagnetic softcopy commands, it causes several tools to "mold" and "shape" the hardcopy, in full three dimensions.

Photographic hardcopy output

Photoplotted hardcopy output covers the bottom portion of Figure 5.6. At the left-most edge is found the versatile filing system of computer output to microfilm. Film size can be the 35-millimeter aperture card, 105-millimeter negatives, or 105-millimeter microfiche. Images are created by exciting a high-resolution CRT with vector graphic or raster-scan techniques and then photoimaging onto silver-halide emulsions. Current state of the art also provides full-color image capture for filing and presentation purposes.

Videotape recordings (VTR) or videocassette recordings (VCR), often direct from the CRT monitor, capture the screen-by-screen displayed images or can move within and around a single display to provide in a continuous sequence what was actually computed and displayed in steps. The video recordings can be in black and white or full color.

Video recordings are listed as offline hardcopy even though once again the images are actually stored as electromagnetic impulses on a magnetic coated film medium.

For precise VTR, VCR, motion picture animation, and COM, special high-resolution displays with flat projection and color-image separation controls allow slides and transparencies to closely match if not often exceed the quality displayed on the working monitor. Similarly, direct projection of colors, with some separation and filtering techniques, will capture unique tints and hues that otherwise might be lost in translation to electrostatic, ink-jet, or pen plotters.

Ah, the excitement of CADD! In the middle row of the photo-output sequence of Figure 5.6 is motion picture photography. This 16- or 35-millimeter hardcopy technique captures the essence of numerous CADD display stills with animation sequencing. What results is a continuity of views, which in their flow present more relative data, in a more controlled state, than is usually achieved by VTR or VCR. Witness the incredible movies, *TRON, The Last Starfighter,* and of course portions of *Star Trek II.* Imagery can be black and white or color, although color is usually the medium of choice.

Shortcutting the normal hardcopy pen-plot routine, 35-millimeter and other types of cameras can capture display images and transfer the presentation directly or indirectly to slides and overhead transparencies. Effects of CRT monitor screen curvature are usually correctible but often neglected. Glare and other unwanted light is typically blocked by using a very large, tapered lens hood that attaches directly to the CRT.

Photooutput in an optical or laser mode can be considered as a pen plot in which the pen writes with light rather than ink. Also, rather than multiple-size pens, the optical or laser "writing" heads can be focused to a wider or narrower beam as required, or operated in a rasterizing fashion to maximize output. The especially concentrated light *laser* stands for *l*ight *a*mplification by *s*timulated *e*mission of *r*adiation.

Via this realm of photoplotting is found the output for typesetting and various engraving procedures (as well as printed circuit photoresist work). The photooptical output through engineering process photography, using laser imaging with pin-registered formats, allows creation of positives and negatives for later, offline, photoprojection or contact reprographics.[A29]

5.3 Generating Hardcopy Output

CADD altered the typical focus of drafting from a continuously modifiable and thus workable original, hardcopy drawing to a constantly volatile *intelligent drawing database,* which can be reproduced by hard-copy plotting as required and at any convenient size or even in various colors. The plotted hardcopy forms of the previous section give rise to some questions about the specific characteristics of the plot medias used. These media forms must be correlated with the plotter functions.

Figure 5.7 tabulates for comparison purposes the various hardcopy "plot" forms. The term "plot" is used advisedly in that some of the photoplot forms such as COM, videotape, slides, motion pictures, and transparencies are not simply vector or raster plots but rather are literal or electronic photographs of the monitor display output. And further, videotape is a special case in that its television "photograph," which by itself is not viewable as would be motion picture film or slides, is captured on offline magnetic "hardcopy" tape for later retransmission.[A27, A30]

The cross referencing in Figure 5.7 denotes some of the "best-use" plot conditions as "all forms." Limited-use cases and hardcopy plot forms which may prove difficult are noted as "limited." Some categories are labeled as "seldom used" rather than "never used" because someone may still try it and make a limited success of that form of output.

Hardcopy devices known as alphanumeric "letter-quality printers" primarily handle text, not graphics. Their output is normally on bond paper with colors provided by changing the ribbon or tape cartridges. Dot matrix printers can handle both graphics and text but with limited colors, and still the output is normally on bond paper stock.

The four types of pen plotters shown are the most common and versatile hardcopy output devices. When coated media are encountered, ballpoints have been known to indent some surfaces (such as clay-coated stock) and to frequently skip or smear on others. Felt-tip pens typically smear on polyester film and occasionally on vellum media.

The electrostatic image, which is a thin layer of emulsified graphite adhered to a statically charged image area, works best with bond papers because of their relatively rough surface. Likewise, the electrostatic image is poorer on polyester film because the material is smooth and relatively impervious. Ink-jet plotters seem to be able to lay an image down onto most thin, flat substrates.[A28]

Matching points to media

Certain hardcopy plotters provide better output when the pen points are matched with their respective, most favourable media types. Of special concern within these combinations are the relative speeds (actually the acceleration rates) of the plotters matched to the specific pen-tip pressures. Figure 5.8 charts these preferred combinations.[A31]

| | CONTENT | | | MEDIA | | | | |
Form	Text	Graphics	Colors	Bond	Coated	Vellum	Drafting film	Photography film
Printer:								
Letter	All forms	Seldom used	Limited	All forms	Limited	Limited	Limited	Seldom used
Dot matrix	All forms	All forms	Limited	All forms	Limited	Limited	Limited	Seldom used
Pen plot:								
Felt-tip	All forms	All forms	All forms	All forms	All forms	Limited	Seldom used	Seldom used
Ballpoint	All forms	All forms	All forms	All forms	Limited	All forms	Limited	Seldom used
Liquid ink	All forms	All forms	All forms	All forms	Limited	All forms	All forms	Seldom used
Scribe	All forms	All forms	Seldom used	Seldom used	All forms; coated film	Seldom used	Seldom used	Seldom used
Electrostatic	All forms	All forms	All forms	All forms	Seldom used	All forms	Limited	Seldom used
Ink jet	All forms	All forms	All forms	All forms	All forms	All forms	All forms	Seldom used
Photoplot:								
COM	All forms	All forms	Seldom used	Seldom used	Seldom used	Seldom used	Seldom used	All forms
Videotape	All forms	All forms	All forms	Seldom used	Seldom used	Seldom used	Seldom used	Magnetic tape
Slide	All forms	All forms	All forms	Seldom used	Seldom used	Seldom used	Seldom used	All forms
Motion picture	All forms	All forms	All forms	Seldom used	Seldom used	Seldom used	Seldom used	All forms
Transparency	All forms	All forms	All forms	Seldom used	Seldom used	Seldom used	Seldom used	Limited
Light beam	All forms	All forms	Seldom used	Seldom used	Seldom used	Seldom used	Seldom used	All forms
Laser	All forms	All forms	Seldom used	Seldom used	Seldom used	Seldom used	Seldom used	All forms
Electron beam	All forms	All forms	Seldom used	Seldom used	Seldom used	Seldom used	Seldom used	All forms

Figure 5.7 Hardcopy output characteristics.

Vector plot media	Preferred speed (ips)	Tip pressure	PREFERRED PLOTTING INSTRUMENT			
			Ballpoint	Liquid ballpoint	Liquid ink	Felt tip
20-lb bond paper	High	Medium	Preferred	Some problems	Some problems	Suitable
Drafting vellum	High	High	Suitable	Preferred	Preferred	Some problems
Polyester matte film	Slow	Medium to high	Not recommended	Some problems	Preferred	Suitable
Polyester clear film	Slow	Medium	Not recommended	Not recommended	Suitable	Preferred
60-lb clay-coated paper	Medium	High	Some problems	Preferred	Some problems	Suitable

Figure 5.8 Point-to-media selection.

Pressurized ballpoint pens are very fast plotting implements for check-plots on opaque bond paper. The image from ballpoints is often inconsistent, has low density, and does not reproduce very well. Liquid ballpoints, or rolling writers, give a much denser line image and are superior, especially in colors, for use on clay-coated paper stocks.

Technical drafting pens that use liquid inks and plotter points (with strengthened tips to take the lateral accelerations) are best used on quality vellums and polyester matte films. These plotter point tips should be tungsten for wear resistance and "cross-groove" to provide better ink flow. Bond-paper media and clay-coated heavier stocks will tend to clog these liquid-ink pen tips. Clear films often require special ink formulations for proper adherence.[A31]

Felt-tip pens—it used to be considered sacrilegious to "draft" with a felt tip, as they were considered suitable only for sketching and other nonrepro uses—are now becoming the rage, especially for colors and for solid-area fills. Felt tips work on most media except for polyester matte film which severely abrades the tips.

5.4 Working with CADD Hardcopy Output

The plotter with its plotted output, which is considered merely a secondary peripheral to the computer system, may indeed be the primary device of a CADD system. For engineering and architectural purposes, the hardcopy is still what is reproduced and transmitted to all project personnel. The paperless office has not yet arrived. Until it does, maximum efficiency from the plotted CADD hardcopy output is required. Not only must the plots be generated quickly, but also the hardcopy plots must be in a form and format that is usable for the next design process stage.[A27]

Hardcopy output has two primary uses:

1. Review or record filing

2. Further reproduction

Hardcopy plots are most often thought of as being drafted with ballpoint or with technical pen using liquid ink on drafting vellum or polyester drafting film. The intent is that the plotted copies be used as checkplots for direct review and comment and for further high-volume reproduction via diazo and electrostatic reprographics to suit the client's and the project's production needs. Mixing of systems is discussed in Chapter 7.

If a plot is to be a checkplot or is just to be filed, then the plotted image may be best if it is "right-reading" (the image is on the top of the sheet and reads normally). However, if the plotted hardcopy is to be used for further reproduction, the best-functioning image can be obtained from a "backward" or "reverse-reading" plot (the image is reverse-mirror-plotted on the back of the sheet so that it reads normally *through* the sheet).[A32]

A simple reversed-image command in the plot file allows the plotted image to be closest to the diazo emulsion of the blue-line whiteprints, thus creating the best possible quality copies. If the plotter cannot handle this reversed-image command, it may be necessary to copy and then reverse the drawing within the CADD software before creating the plot spool.

On the other hand, plots that will be photographically reproduced should be plotted right-reading so that the image is closest to the camera lens and camera negative emulsion. This also applies to electrostatic copying (xerography).

Experience has shown that most CADD users will plot an average of two to three copies just to get the precise version that they want. This multiple-copy plotting is primarily caused by two factors[A24]:

1. Operator's mistake in selecting the incorrect plot mode:
   a. Full-size when half-size was desired
   b. Too few or too many layers
   c. Incorrect logical pen function, width, or color

2. Plotter's (plus operator's) mistake in function:
   a. Pen skipping or clogging
   b. Toner streaking or fade-out
   c. Too heavy or too light pen pressure

Format plotting

CADD drawings can be generated with or without border formats. If the plotter media is preprinted drawing formats, wasted sheets caused by the plotter's (actually the operator's) errors could prove to be a formidable expense. It would seem absurd for the conventional drafter to throw away a printed format each time an error was made or a minor revision was required.[A24]

Plotting on a format is especially valid for checkplotting, where only the heart of the drawing need be plotted. Plotting on a format can save the tedious replotting of the rather involved format lines and text and logos which are necessary for the "final" production plots. Unfortunately, these quick plots and checkplots are precisely where the printed-format-eating errors occur.

Reprographic systems drafting and reproduction services to the rescue! Figure 5.9 diagrams the logic for creating full-size and half-size reproductions of the *format only*. Plotting is then done on the reproductions, which can be readily trashed as new issues are generated.

From the one printed-format original can be made electrostatic vellums, erasable sepia vellums, and matte films, along with simple direct-print blue lines and black lines. If reverse-reading plots are to be created, format reproductions should obviously also be made reverse reading.

For half-size or other convenient-size plotting purposes, electrostatic vellum reductions allow further creation of erasable film and vellum sepias or whiteprints for checkplotting. For the best-quality reductions (or enlargements), use simple photorestorations of the original format via negative onto clear polyester film to create half-size sepia or whiteprint copies for plotting.

Repligraphics

This term takes "repli" from replication, the speed of copying within a CADD system, and "graphics" from the high technologies of reprographics systems to make a synergistic composite concept and set of methodologies. Using repligraphics, which deals primarily in CADD hardcopy handling, the productivity of CADD can be maintained and in some cases even enhanced.[A10]

Repligraphics provides an advantage in giving thought to how the plot will be used *before generating the plot.* For example, if a drawing is plotted at half-size and then photographically restored onto moist-

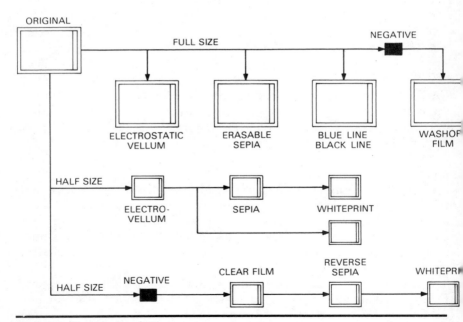

Figure 5.9 Formats for plotting.

erasable ("wash-off") polyester matte-surfaced drafting film at the full original size, not only are the plot vector distances reduced by a factor of 4 (one-half of each principal direction) but also the final wash-off drafting film is manually workable for any last-minute or off-the-CADD-system changes and additions.

This situation is echoed in the fast electrostatic raster plots. The best electrostatic plots are created on opaque bond paper, which is usually too opaque to make direct diazo reproductions. Here again, the high-quality, fast CADD plot can be photorestored onto translucent wash-off film for both workability and reproducibility. Or the raster plot can be electrostatically copied onto vellum media.

After the production plots have been created for use in making large-volume copies for construction or fabrication phase submittals, a very sharp plot can be made with multi-colored felt-tip pens on 60- or 80-pound clay-coated bond paper for display purposes. In some cases, these multicolored plots have a sharpness of image that can be recaptured for additional copying. Color-imaged raster-format plots in the very fast techniques of ink jet and color electrostatics might be used to capture the polychrome design images or merely to get the most hardcopy production out the fastest.

Current state of the art are the optical light and especially laser light-beam photoplots. Driven by the CADD plot file, these registered and layered small-size negatives are being used to recreate formats and individual layers and composite plots. These CADD-plotted negatives are subsequently used in a process photoprojector system to create full-size, or any convenient-size, workable "originals" at a fraction of the plot time throughout. In addition, the separate but registered layer negatives can be used to generate intermediate sizes of negatives for creating the plates for color offset.

And all you really wanted was to get *something* out of your CADD system to show at a meeting with a client in 1 hour! There is the bottom line in CADD: hardcopy output to satisfy a need. Maybe the first step in acquiring a CADD system should be to ask: What are its hardcopy output capabilities? What kind? How soon?[A27]

Contending with tomorrow

The standards discussed in Section 5.1 culminate in the hardcopy output forms that are ultimately handled physically. If certain standards were set for display of the CADD software database, perhaps the subsequent hardcopy output would communicate better. Unfortunately, many of the plotter vendors and manufacturers do not as yet match these standards for lines and colors. Not only do they not match established industry standards, but also they are not mutually compatible.

Preliminary discussions on this subject were printed in 1985 in the article "Display to Plot to Repro."[A26] The essence of this problem can be stated as follows: The red line displayed by CADD is not the same color red as the line that is plotted by felt-tip, nor is it the same red as plotted by pressurized ballpoint or rolling writer, nor is it even the same red as the liquid ink in technical pens.

The same problem holds generally true for the other basic colors: yellow, blue, brown, green, orange, and purple. In addition, the offset colors (magenta, cyan, yellow, and black) used by electrostatic, ink-jet, and laser-imaging devices are often not directly echoed by the software-supported displays.

These "minor" problems should be given some consideration at the point of acquisition of a CADD system. The resolution of these hardcopy imaging problems may not be possible, yet, with any but a very small number of CADD systems.

6

Output Filing
and Maintenance

Now that we have created all this CADD imagery, what is to be done with it? What constitutes the archival "master" or "original" of the CADD system's drawings? Where is the "master drawing file" in the system? How is this master file created, accessed, and protected? The rate at which both discrete and interrelated files are generated within a CADD system is awesome. These files are not only within the CADD system, but also they reside in numerous offline softcopy and hardcopy forms. This is the housekeeping chapter, possibly not exciting, but necessary for proper CADD system health and well-being.

When archival filing is considered, the saved "master" (either the "original" or a copy) must exist in a recallable form for the duration of the liability limits of the documents for the particular project. For near-term filing, the concept is to save the "original master" images for reference and for reuse. Traditionally, the master drawings are the manually created sheets. Similarly, the master drawings could be considered the CADD plotted hardcopy, the electronically drafted "originals." But this may neglect the viability of the CADD database.

The following statement has been made: "The hardcopy is the master, not the drawing on the CAD system."[A33] Compare this with the similar concept, from pin graphics, that the final composite is the master, not the bases and overlays used to create the composite drawing. Within these ideas there may be two divergent understandings of what constitutes the master.

One CADD concept, A, is that the images stored within the CADD system database do in fact constitute the master file from which, from time to time, plot files are created which in turn allow hardcopies to be generated for proper distribution. Taken to one of its conclusions, this "stored-master" concept implies ease of access, revision, and recall at any time, electronically, without the encumbrance of hardcopy files. This is one of the logic points of the electronic office—that the data is always in a volatile or dynamic state.

The second CADD concept, B, holds that the computer-assisted interactive graphic system is merely a very efficient tool in the creation of construction and fabrication documents (hardcopy). It is this hardcopy that must be further copied and, as usual, distributed offline. From this standpoint the CADD system could be looked upon as a rapid-electronic-drafter-with-memory which might leave (be magnetically erased), and so the plotted output is considered the only real master—something solid that you can hang on to. The logic here is a reminder of the need to back up all computer files in case of accidental loss of memory or other operational error.

Compare CADD concept A with the pin graphics method of considering the bases and overlays as the true master drawing layers from which composite copies can be made and distributed at any time. Special file replicates or repligraphic copies would be small-format, pin-registered negatives. As with CADD files, these repligraphic negatives only capture the data at some point frozen in time, while the original layered masters continue to be updated and reissued.

The alternate CADD concept, B, matches the pin graphics idea that the bases and overlays are only present to ease the creation of the composite. It is, after all, the composite which is signed, sealed, and copied for proper distribution. After the composite master is created, it becomes the primary (offline) vehicle for any further changes. And, therefore, any negatives, intermediates, software files, or original bases and overlays may be conveniently discarded or salvaged for other data-bases and projects.[A33]

Filing copies

Fortunately or unfortunately, we tend to keep records. As this relates to construction and fabrication drawings, records are kept of significant design stages, special client-review issues and comments, major bid and construction or fabrication releases, and occasionally as a record of as-built approximations.

In the case of U.S. Department of Defense requirements, and similar archival standards, these records must be kept (and maintained for the 20- to 40-year project life). This must be done at each significant point in the design-construction process so that an audit trail is clearly established. Using the National Fire Protection Association (NFPA) as a reference source,[B22] the general control over records could be established for at leat four classes;

1. Vital records

2. Important records

3. Useful records

4. Nonessential records

Enter CADD. To hold to the above procedures, a hardcopy is made (plotted), duplicated, filed, and distributed to and for all concerned parties at each pertinent step in the design process. In some cases, additional softcopy records are also maintained. Alternates, estimates, revisions, addenda, and scope changes all must also be formatted to plot file, plotted, copied, and distributed. Should these records be maintained for a CADD system as softcopy or as hardcopy? Should these classes of records be further considered as dynamic and "volatile," meaning currently recallable, or as "nonvolatile," meaning that they are for off-system reference only?

Plotting to tapes or disks cannot currently be consider permanent. Therefore, archival plotting must be via laser graphics and micrographics to photographic film, or via electrostatic raster-scan plotters to paper, vellum, or polyester film, or via vector pen plots to paper, vellum, or polyester film. This hardcopy plotted output from CADD can now be considered for the various copying and permanent filing purposes.

Micrographics is the most versatile filing system, and hence computer output to microfilm may be the most efficient filing method. All the other hardcopy output media must be handled as if they were "hand-drawn, master originals." They may require micrographics as well as reprographics for restoration before copying or filing. Plus, these myriad hardcopies require just plain file space.[A34]

Thus, any consideration of filing CADD hardcopy starts with the understanding that the CADD hardcopy, unless it is in a micrographic format, is the same as hand-drawn work—except that there may be more of it, it may be more colorful, and it certainly will be generated at a faster pace.

6.1 Electronic Filing

CADD drawings are created electronically, reside as electromagnetically charged relationships, are displayed as electromagnetic pulses, and are filed electronically as softcopy. Since this form of existence is so easily altered (the relationships of the charged bits can be easily scrambled or lost altogether), it is necessary to provide viable backup soft and hard copies.

Because of the dynamic or volatile nature of the CADD database, special precautions and security measures must be applied, depending upon the importance of the data records. Initially, CADD drawings appear as electronic images on the monitor-CRT display screen. This displayed image is supported by local dynamic random access memory, and it would disappear if system power were lost or even momentarily interrupted. For this reason, the CADD image must be periodically filed, stored, or "saved" to a more permanent condition on floppy disk, hard disk, magnetic tape, or laser disk.[A35]

The current or active drawing that is being displayed and interacted with must be periodically filed or saved. Likewise, the entire project and system files must be properly stored, in duplicate, to assure database integrity.

Backup procedures

The immediate, or current, CADD drawings database on disk or tape is also in jeopardy of loss of data or of being overwritten by new data. To assure controlled continuity of the database, extra copies of the primary database are created and stored offline to the CADD system.

Figure 6.1 provides a chart of the method for creating a backup file that is current to within 24 hours. Normal CADD system usage does the following: immediate data exists on the workstation disk file, and any work done to that file and subsequently refiled will overwrite existing data. This may be what is intended; it is too bad if it is not intended, for the change is permanent. For security against loss of workforce (operator) time, the previous day's data need not be lost if it still resides in the backup system.

Some CADD systems provide, and others should be modified to provide, an immediate backup or "OOPS!" command which allows cancellation of the last previous command and reinstatement of the immediately prior condition. Without this short-term control, efficiency of system use may be degraded. Or, at worst, valuable time and data could be lost.

Backup files

The hierarchy for setting up a backup file begins with the "parent" master file, which could be the "current" file or the initial backup disk or tape. The subsequent backup disks or tapes of the same, or a revised, database become the "child" of the previous master file. The next backup series creates a new "child" which changes the previous "child" to the new "parent" and the old, initial "parent" master file to the "grandparent."[B1, p. 957]

If there were no sequencing control over file backup procedures, the child, parent, grandparent, great-grandparent, etc., would generate an ever-increasing stack of disks or tapes. However, if you stay as close as possible to the initial parent-child sequence, approximately 15 disks or tapes should be capable of covering at least 12 months of work, with optimal backup coverage to well within 24 hours.

In the sequence shown in Figure 6.1, a tape or disk backup is made of each day's work. Then, on a prearranged day, usually a Saturday or Sunday, an extra backup disk or tape is made to cover the entire week's efforts. The next Monday's backup procedure writes over the preceding Monday's tape or disk file, and so on for each sequential day throughout the week.

A completely new backup disk or tape is created to cover the work of week 2. The next 2 weeks of Monday through Sunday tape over their respective previous disks or tapes, followed by a separate disk or tape for weeks 3 and 4. After the fourth (or fifth) week, a disk or tape is created for the first month. Then the sequence starts anew, overwriting the daily and weekly disks or tapes and creating a backup file for the second month. Another series of tapes is initiated to cover each of at least 3 successive months. "Month ?" suits project conditions or serves

Backup mode	Functional time frame	Daily file	Weekly file	Monthly file	Annual file
Daily	Monday	B-1			
	Tuesday	B-2			
	Wednesday	B-3			
	Thursday	B-4			
	Friday	B-5			
	Saturday	B-6			
	Sunday	B-7			
Weekly	Week 1		W-1		
	Week 2		W-2		
	Week 3		W-3		
	Week 4		W-4		
Monthly	Month 1			M-1	
	Month 2			M-2	
	Month 3			M-3	
	Month ?			M-?	
Project	Annual 1				A-1

Figure 6.1 Backup file sequencing.

as a semiannual backup until the project, or at least an annual record of the database, is filed.

Some firms shorten this effort, and thus lessen their backup capability, by initiating a full backup of the database *only weekly*. These backups can cover specific projects or the entire database including the CADD software programs.

As a reminder, taking a page from most computer systems and CADD vendors' manuals, the primary CADD software should not be used as the "working master." All actual project work, and especially any modifications to the CADD software system programming, should be done on a backup copy or copies of the original software set or sets.

Partial backup

For some sophisticated CADD systems, the backup procedure is not a complete refiling of the entire database but rather an *incremental backup* that compares the backup tape with the current database and seeks out and revises only those elements of the database which have changed since the previous backup. This procedure takes far less time than a complete backup, but the sophistication usually is not available on microCADD systems.

The incremental backup is often used on a daily basis in order to limit the amount of offline time needed to accomplish the backup. The complete backup procedure is normally accomplished on weekends or at other times when there is the least amount of user activity. This incremental backup can even be a specific command-initiated "phantom" or unseen, unnoticed program which does the backup procedure at preset intervals but only during those times when the CPU is not otherwise being accessed.

Determine which backup procedures are recommended for and available on your CADD system. Review how the consistent implementation of these procedures would fit within your CADD production practices. The true reminder of how often you should "back up" for your particular activity levels will occur when, for some reason, you lose some valuable, or at least time-consuming, data which must be completely regenerated because there was no backup available.

Layered filing

A common concept for CADD and repro-systems drafting is: share and reuse the common data. Data that has been generated, digitized, or scanned into the CADD database is replicated (copied) into new files and onto new project sheets for reuse. This data may have been rescaled and even slightly revised to "fit" the new configurations, or it could be simply a copied layer or layers.

Figure 6.2 shows reusable data elements as blocks labeled 1 through 9. However, rather than just being isolated "copy-move" elements, these blocks represent entire layers of shared data. Pin graphics provides for mechanical registration of these shared layers, while CADD handles the X-Y orientation alignment of the layers with binary digits and electromagnetic registration.[A26]

Unfortunately, Figure 6.2 also indicates that these shared layers may have been rather "semipermanently copied" onto other sheet files. Layers 1, 2, and 3 are shared or copied into "Sheet File B" as background for layer 5. Similarly, layers 1 and 2 are also copied into files C, D, and E. And special layer 6 has been copied into file D from file C. This may be fine if the shared layers do not require further revision.

If revisions are required to layers 1, 2, 3, and 6, then some additional recopying may be required in order to assure that all the common or shared background layers maintain data integrity. In pin graphics, this would be in the hardcopy form of "slicks," "throwaways," or film negatives. CADD systems, on the other hand, merely replace each entire layer electronically—if the referenced shared elements and their respective sheet files are remembered. In all cases, care must be taken to "edit" the remaining unique layers in each sheet file to assure compatibility with the revised shared layers.[A26]

Don't file twice

Figure 6.3 provides an alternative, though completely consistent with either pin graphics or CADD, logic process to that of Figure 6.2. In Figure 6.2, the shared layers are copied to or resident in each separate sheet file. Effectively, Figure 6.2 shows a requirement for "storing" 19 layers of unique and shared data.

Figure 6.3 delineates the more efficient form, especially with regard to CADD, for shared layer use by keeping *all the interrelated nine layers*

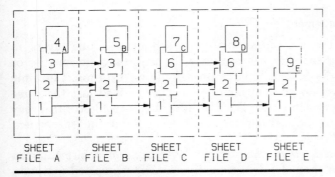

Figure 6.2 Shared data elements.

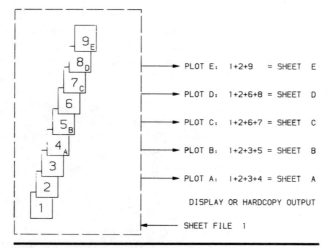

PLOT E: 1+2+9   = SHEET E

PLOT D: 1+2+6+8 = SHEET D

PLOT C: 1+2+6+7 = SHEET C

PLOT B: 1+2+3+5 = SHEET B

PLOT A: 1+2+3+4 = SHEET A

DISPLAY OR HARDCOPY OUTPUT

SHEET FILE 1

Figure 6.3 Don't store the same layer twice.

in one and the same file. File-use efficiency in this figure has a minimum 19:9 factor over that in Figure 6.2, which may be further increased by eliminating the operator handling, codification, and backup time requirements for multiple files.

Output from Figure 6.2 or Figure 6.3 is to a display monitor or to the plot queue. In either case, the output of any given sheet (sheet A = layers 1+2+3+4, sheet B = layers 1+2+3+5, etc.) is the sum of its specific unique and shared parts.

By loading the complete file 1, from Figure 6.3, to the CADD monitor with a sequential control over which layers are "ON" or "OFF," sheets A through E can be displayed separately for ongoing work. Revisions to a given layer do not require extensive copying and codification to other sheet files, but the correlated disciplines' unique layer revisions must still be done.

Database file management

Depending upon the amount of data on each of the nine layers in Figure 6.3, loading time for the complete file may be quite lengthy or may even exceed the RAM limits of the CADD workstation. Certainly it would take longer to load all nine layers than to load just the three or four required for each sheet. But the advantages in file control may outweigh the agony of waiting for file loading (and the subsequent "saving" of time).

In the transition from normal, simple layer and composite filing in manual systems to that of fully productive CADD-supported methods, a basic understanding of file handling with database management principles is necessary. For a complete discussion of these concepts, refer to Foley and Van Dam[B13] and to Raker and Rice.[B14] The database management concepts will handle the nine shared layers and five composite sheets of Figures 6.2 and 6.3 not as groups of layers but rather as related elements.[B10]

Each layer, 1 through 9, could be filed separately in the database but each would be "tagged" with an "attribute" of or relationship with the corresponding sheet or sheets. Thus, when sheet A is recalled from the database, those layers tagged with the "Sheet A" relational attribute are loaded to the terminal monitor. Similarly with all other sheets. As in the example in Figure 6.3, only nine layers need be filed. However, all nine layers need not be loaded in order to recall a related sheet.

Now, scale up from 9 layers to 1024+ and from 5 sheets to 125 drawings, and the efficiency of filing with database management becomes quite clear. Next, add selected plan segments, reusable details, intelligent lines, intelligent text, and common symbols (in library formats) to this relational database. The monitor images and subsequent plot images of the drawings need not be considered as discrete, whole entities but rather as the selected sum of the related parts. This is the future of computer-aided design and drafting. It is here now.

6.2 Revising and Retrieving Electronic Output

It seems a simple process to create a CADD drawing and then to file that drawing. When revisions are necessary, the specific drawing can be recalled from the database. Figure 6.4 steps through this sequence of events to further show that the recalled drawing can be revised and then refiled into the database. For some systems, this procedure to "save" or "file" data is a periodic, automatic function beyond the normal control of the CADD operator.

Then the problems crop up. Oops! That was a mistake: the revision to the drawing was not complete or possibly was not required. However, by refiling, "saving" the revised sheet back into the database, *the existing drawing's contents were lost because they were overwritten!* The damage has been done, permanently.

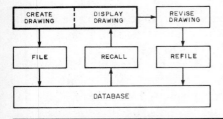

Figure 6.4 Direct filing may be dangerous.

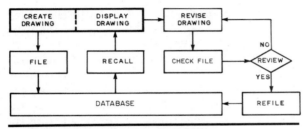

Figure 6.5 Indirect filing may be helpful.

There is probably no use in attempting to reclaim the original imagery (unless certain OOPS! or undo commands or other backup procedures are in place). Plus, this type of error could be committed unintentionally by inadvertently giving a new sheet the same name as the "original master" in file; or the error could, unfortunately, have been intentional.

As an alternative to this scenario, Figure 6.5 uses a similar procedure but includes *an intermediate checking file* which intercepts the revised sheet before it is inserted into the formal database. This procedure allows a checker or project manager the opportunity to review the work before formal acceptance is made.

The drafter or operator implied in Figure 6.5 would have the access rights to recall *a copy of a specific project sheet* and to make revisions to that copy (which may have the same name). However, the hidden commands of the CADD software could direct any subsequent filing of the drawing to an interim holding bin for checking before formal filing. The operator can retrieve a drawing, create new drawings, and make modifications to existing drawings but is constrained from replacing or overwriting valuable data without additional approvals.

6.3 Plot-File Maintenance

A drawing is initiated on the CADD system by addressing a file, displaying a format on the CRT, and commencing with interactive graphics. As work progresses, the drawing is routinely and frequently saved by copying it to the main file or to an interim file. When a hardcopy plot is required of a particular drawing, a separate command is initiated which takes the displayed data, translates or reformats the image commands for the specific plotter, and files the data in a plot queue or plot file separately from the master file.

Figure 6.6 shows the sequence for creating this plot file. This function has often been known as "creating the plot spool," because early CADD systems loaded, or spooled, the plotter-formatted data onto streaming tape. Regardless of the location of the plot file, on disk or tape, it is from the plot file that the plotter receives its directions. This seems to be a very straightforward means for obtaining a hardcopy.

Unfortunately the "handshake" required to translate CADD systems data into a form usable for plotting varies for different plotters. Just as simple daisy wheel and dot matrix printers require that their dual in-line pin (DIP)[B1] switches be set in a proper sequence, so also there are necessary software controller interfaces for each plotter. Figure 6.7 tabulates some of the plotter handshake languages currently being used.

These plotter or printer controller protocols must be verified between the host CPU and the plotter controllers. The two systems must speak the same language *consistently* in order to achieve proper hardcopy plot output. While most of the well-known CADD systems are supported by the plotter vendors, some CADD systems are selectively formatted to interface with only one plotter format. And unfortunately, some upgrades and extensive revisions to some CADD programs may neglect to incorporate these handshakes. What used to work easily now requires

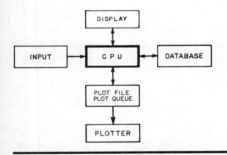

Figure 6.6 Plot file, then the plot.

Plotter supplier	Software Operating Program for Plotter Controller	
	Online	Offline
Benson	CS800	CS800
CalComp	907, 951, 960	918, 922, 925
Gerber Scientific	Gerber	Gerber
Hewlett-Packard	HP-GL	HP-GL
Houston Instruments	HIPLOT, DM/PL	HIPLOT, DM/PL
Nicolet Zeta	Zeta Standard	Zeta Standard
Tektronix	PLOT 10	PLOT 10
Versatec	Versaplot	Versaplot
Xynetics	C84	C82

Figure 6.7 Plotter controller systems.

some reconfiguring of the plotter protocols for proper output. These conditions must be clarified before the full system is brought online.

Online, offline

In anticipation of Chapter 7 and following up on the concepts of Chapter 3, the sharing of the CADD database does not end with the simple sharing of the CADD project files. Occasionally just the plot spool or plot file needs to be shared. This sharing of the plot file is normally considered to be offline: strictly separate and operating apart from the original host CADD system. Other plot-file configurations might be used only in the online condition: being directly driven by or under the control of the original host CADD system or a similar system.

The distinction between "online" and "offline" is very important for the interface or use of a plot file between two CADD systems. For example, a CADD plot file configured under the online protocols of CalComp 907 will be excellent for the direct host driving of the plotter. However, this CC907 configured plot file will not be compatible for offline use, whereas the CalComp 925 format is compatible offline.

Before initiating a CADD system, determine whether the output from the CADD system is to be shared or serviced offline as well as online and whether the necessary plotter-controller software sets are resident within the system.

Proper plot configuration

Figure 6.8 carries forward the logic of Figure 6.6 while inserting the specific plot-file-initiating commands to configure the file for online or

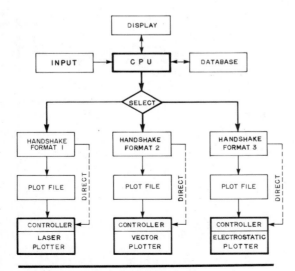

Figure 6.8 Configured plot files.

offline, or vector or raster, hardcopy output. Rather than merely issuing the command PLOT CURRENT, there should be a prior thought and an extra step taken—the command PLOT, PLOT-SHARE, or PLOT-RASTER or a similar directive which calls forth specific macros or other command sequences required to initiate the proper formatting of the plot file or files.

The online plot file could be vectorized or rasterized depending upon the onsite CADD system plotting equipment. Similarly, the offline plot file could be vectorized or rasterized depending upon how the service bureau or interfacing consultant intends to use the data. Figure 6.8 presents only few of the possible plot-file combinations.

If only a single plotter device is on your system, these configurations may seem unimportant; the plot control sequence may seem to be "direct" (and it may even lock up the terminal until the plot is completed). However, as your system expands or your database is networked, these tweakings of the plot-spool configurations will be required to assure coherent "de-spooling" for each output device.

6.4 Hardcopy Filing

When CADD gets around to hardcopy, it essentially becomes a drafter, an electrographer, and most efficiently, a photographer. It does each of these chores quite well and certainly far faster than the human drafter. However, what CADD the plotter does most is to *generate a lot more* hardcopy "masters" than is normally done manually. These myriads of "original documents" can accumulate even more rapidly and ominously than the CADD backup filing systems noted in Section 6.1.

All the CADD hardcopy forms noted in Figure 5.6 must be filed or thrown out, depending upon their overall importance to the project. Probably the best advice would be to throw out more of them. Barring that, the next best option is to record the hardcopy images on microfilm to save space, and then throw out the hardcopies themselves.

Continuing from the basic concept in Figure 6.6, the hardcopy output from the plotter forms can be separated into the four basic categories. Figure 6.9 first shows that the electronic (softcopy) file can be considered as having two forms: (1) the dynamic or current working file and (2) the backup file or duplicate copy of the database. Then Figure 6.9 shows the four major categories for hardcopy.[B22] These can be considered and handled as follows:

Vital records. Vital records are irreplaceable sets of drawings and alphanumeric data sheets, as well as those in which a reproduced copy would not have as great a value as the original. Documents which would be necessary to rebuild, repair, or reconstitute a product or facility are also vital records.

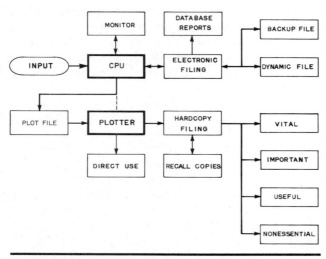

Figure 6.9 Hardcopy filing.

Vital hardcopy should be stored in a fireproof, waterproof, and ver- minproof environment, usually off-site from the original database. For CADD systems, the primary vital record might be the softcopy database, as discussed previously. However, the vital CADD hardcopy may be interim design stages that were signed off, presentation color imagery that has since been modified, videotape and motion picture images of sequential events, and the end-of-project hardcopy plots that capture the last-instance configurations. All these forms that are *vital to the business of the project* should be protected.

Important records. Important records are sets of drawings and alpha- numeric data sheets which would be difficult or time-consuming to replace, as well as those in which the reproduction of a copy in usable, workable form would be considered very costly. These documents would only be necessary to further clarify details or other backup data con- cerning the vital records for the product or facility.

Important hardcopy should be, but does not have to be, stored in a fireproof, waterproof, and verminproof environment, usually off-site from the original database. For CADD systems, the important hardcopy records might be the alternate design schemes, alternate FEM analysis, designer-engineer-client comments, and standard detail or subsystem images that would be used for offline copy, cut, and tape drafting or reference. All these forms that are *important in the avoidance of delay to the business of the project* should be protected.

Useful records. Useful records are those sets of drawings and alpha- numeric data sheets which would be inconvenient or only moderately time-consuming to recreate, or which could be easily reproduced into workable forms. These documents are marginally necessary to maintain the continuity of an ongoing project. This is the first level which could be lost and not pose any real hindrance to the CADD-supported project.

Useful hardcopy should be allotted a specific short-term file space which could be on-site and would be periodically purged to remove nonessential, nonuseful documents. For CADD systems, the useful hardcopy records might be the software programming modifications and clarification hardcopies, checkplots, scale-reference plots, three-dimensional wire-frame perspective or massing studies used as the basis for offline presentation work, and facility detail or subsystem images that would be used for offline engineering or design discussions. All these forms that are *useful in the ongoing business of the project* should be periodically purged. Certain documents in this class might be upgraded to "important" during the periodic reviews. No special protection other than normal caution and handling need be considered.

Nonessential records. Nonessential records are those sets of drawings and alphanumeric data sheets which are only a short-term convenience or are an interim form and format used to reprographically create "final" copies or other workable forms. These documents should be handled in a constructive manner such that immediately after their short-term convenience and usefulness is ended, they are discarded or recycled. This level of documents should be actively purged so as to avoid accumulation which would form a fire hazard.

Nonessential hardcopies are the bane of CADD systems. Usually they take the form of full and partial documents and plots that were intended to be useful but failed to achieve their intended level of quality. These nonessential CADD system records are all around you—throw them out! Or turn them over and plot on the reverse side.

6.5 Revising and Retrieving Hardcopy Output

One of the first rules in CADD systems is "Do not revise or otherwise modify the hardcopy!" The hardcopy could be considered only an interim record of the status of the design database. Any revisions to the hardcopy, without simultaneous or matching revision to the CADD database, could jeopardize the integrity of the database.

However, based upon the discussions in Section 3.3 and 3.4, there are many times when minor or even major manual drafting and other modifications may be valid on the hardcopy. Further, the reviser's intention may be to enter these revisions into the database at a later date. The simplest example of this condition is the issuance of a workable checkplot to an offline designer or engineer, who makes modifications to the plot, issues copies for further review, and then accumulates and

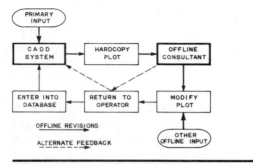

Figure 6.10 Revisions to hardcopy plots.

consolidates the revisions before returning the plot to the CADD operator for incorporation into the project database.

Figure 6.10 charts this flow path from the ongoing CADD project database through hardcopy output to offline consultors. The modifications are then returned via the CADD system operator to the project database. The alternate route, shown with dotted lines, indicates very immediate feedback from the offline checker directly to the operator for entry into the database. This secondary shortcut path often engenders a quick reissuance of the slightly revised database as a new hardcopy plot which may be better suited for offline review.

Reentry of the revisions to the database which were marked on the plotted hardcopy can be accomplished as directly generated interactive graphics using design and drafting input commands. Or, if the revisions are relatively accurate, they may be entered by digitizing or scanning the new information.

Typically, the above procedures are thought of as two-dimensional efforts, entering lines and text revisions from two-dimensional plotted originals or reproductions. With the advent of sonic digitizers, magnetic transduction techniques, and vidicon capture of projected light beams,[A36] three-dimensional solid hardcopy—molded or sculpted forms—can be revised by machine or manual means and then the revisions entered into the CADD database.

Retrieval to where?

Direct entry of the generated or digitized revision data may be harmful to the project database if it is unrefined or incomplete, or if it includes potential errors. For this reason, it may be wise to set aside one or more layers on each project drawing for reception of revision input. After the "new" data is entered, it can be checked and edited by interactive graphics before or during the inclusion of the modifications to the project documents. In some cases, this modification effort may lead to the creation of a new project document while still retaining the original drawing in its prerevision status.

Figure 6.11 traces the logic path from the project file in the database to the hardcopy plot via terminal commands by the operator. Offline comments may be returned directly to the operator or may be incorporated into the two- or three-dimensional hardcopy. Revision and modification data is reentered into a designated revision layer by the CADD system operator.

After all the revision information has been gathered, it can be interactively edited by the operator for incorporation into the project file. Taking a cue from "Color Word Processing" by Andrew Lippman and associates,[A37] revisions to the database may be displayed in a prominent color and on a discrete layer until all applications have been addressed and the disciplines have signed off.

This cautionary extra step may help to hold unharmed a project database that otherwise might lose its integrity. This extra step, including the digitizing or revision layer, also allows electronic and optical scanning of whole, or complete, document sets of revisions in an en masse format. The subsequent operator-controlled interaction allows setting relational database attributes to the revision's lines and text to facilitate report generation.

Revising the hardcopy

Lest we forget, most forms of plotted hardcopy are very similar to manual drafting methods and media. (Refer to Section 5.3.) As such,

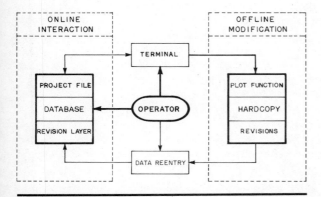

Figure 6.11 Revision layer holding bin.

manual revisions to the hardcopy would follow the normal rules of drafting or machining. Experience has shown us that these offline revisions are probably not as accurate nor as uniform as those generated by the computer and its plotter. Thus, any electronic recapturing of the hardcopy add-on revision data will be prone to error and therefore require extra control.

Alternative Parallel
Approaches

If not CADD, then what? And with CADD, what else? More explicitly, how do one or more CADD workstations fit into a professional architectural, engineering, or manufacturing design office? The transition to CADD implies movement from a position of creating contract or fabrication drawings completely with manual and reprographic techniques to a position where some CADD hardware and software are added to the current mix, and thence to the ever-increasing use of CADD.

Rarely does the CADD system completely supplant the ongoing manual methods. The closest current approach to the creation of a primarily electronic design and drafting office seems to have occurred in one- and two-person architectural and engineering firms where the principal is the designer and the drafter and the presenter. Most of the hardcopy creations in these firms are generated by the plotter after having been initiated on the CADD workstation. The hardcopy output then is typically reproduced into presentable and workable form before final finishing touches are applied manually using precision drafting equipment.

For the remainder of CADD systems users, the firm size usually dictates a modest one to four CADD workstations installed as high-tech assistance in the development of a project. The typical total staff size varies between 5 and 50 people. Therefore, after proper CADD system acquisition, the real transition step is in how to mix CADD with the non-CADD design process and drafting output methods.

A great deal of the primary logic and application of computer-aided design and drafting systems was covered in Chapters 2 and 3. Here we will explore alternate drafting methods as they parallel the use of CADD systems and especially as they *use CADD input and output intermittently* in the process of completing the drafting communication for a project.

These alternative parallel approaches do not negate the use of CADD, but rather they are intended to show the myriad practical applications for CADD and its hardcopy output. The traditional manual drafting, systems drafting, and advanced reprographics techniques can be enhanced by using CADD support. More important, the hardcopy output from CADD is also greatly enhanced by the direct applications of manual systems drafting, reprographics, and repligraphics.

7.1 What to Do with What Is Not CADD

In Chapter 3, the discussion of Figure 3.10 presented a situation in which the CADD system might be used for creating 35 to 65 percent of the project documents. If this were the case, then what would be done, what methods would be used, with the remaining 65 to 35 percent of the drawings? They at least must be completed by hand.

This situation is primarily governed by considerations based upon the hardcopy output from CADD. Specifically, the output from the vector and raster plotters affects the system's application. Input to CADD is not necessarily involved, but the configuration of the CADD workstation and thus its response and prompts to the operator are vitally important. These output concerns are:

1. CADD the drafter is more precise and more consistent in line work and especially lettering quality than manual efforts.

2. CADD the drafter is fundamentally faster than the manual alternatives.

3. CADD the drafter's hardcopy output may not be directly suitable for further drafting or reproduction.

Matching standards

Based upon these considerations, the acquisition and implementation of even a single (micro) CADD workstation in a design and drafting office may put very strong pressure on the adherence to, or the adoption of and then adherence to, office drafting standards.[B11] The precision quality of CADD as plotter or drafter will normally put to shame all previous manual drafting output unless the manual methods include extensive ink drafting with standard lettering guides and the use of lettering systems (tapes, rub-ons, etc.).

Figure 7.1 compares the traditional manual drafting methodology with the use of *repligraphic drafting:* the mixing of CADD with manual and repro-systems techniques. The traditional manual drafting efforts include the establishment of office standards for drafting but unfortunately do not always include the adoption and consistent enforcement of those standards. The traditional manual drafting standards are more often used as a reference system rather than necessarily as a day-to-day way of doing things.

Then the controlled display and plotted hardcopy of CADD are added to the mix. Standard drafting procedures, line weights, text (font) shapes, and text heights begin to be enforced. The enforcer may typically be the ultimate client (rather than merely the production chief) who abhors the comparatively lousy manual efforts and is enthralled by the visual impact (not necessarily the design integrity) of the CADD plots.

However, CADD is also impacted by these office standards. If the manual drafter must match the consistency of CADD the drafter, at least the CADD system should come close to matching the established standard techniques which are available to and applied by the manual drafter. Refer to Section 5.1 for detailed examples of proper configurations for the repligraphic drafter.

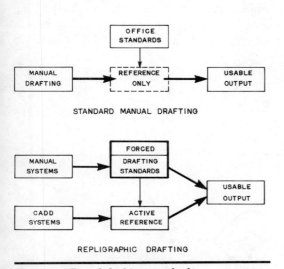

Figure 7.1 Forced drafting standards.

Matching speed

Don't try. The speed of the CADD system's plotter is not to be matched manually. Even a vector-driven pen plotter that has been slowed down to minimal acceleration will quickly outdistance the experienced manual drafter. CADD will beat "John Henry." But the system can be out-flanked.

Actually, when properly used, a CADD system is not in competition with the manual drafter. Certain drawings or portions of drawings will be assigned to the CADD system, and the remainder will be handled manually. The only reason speeds need be "matched" to the established proper project production management, is so that the manually drafted portions of the project can be completed in a timely conjunction with the completion and plotting of the CADD-supported portions.

Figure 7.2 shows the very simplified paralleling of production output from CADD and that of manual systems where their differentials in speed are translated into total time-on-system values. Note that the culmination of the CADD effort occurs at some discrete Δx time *before* the end of the manual effort. This final segment of time at least allows for the signing and sealing of all project hardcopy before reproduction and distribution.

As is demonstrated in actual practice, the utilization of CADD systems is often that of an *on-stream,* then *off-stream* relationship with a continuous manual drafting effort. Since not all the project documents are on the computer, and because of CADD's great speed and efficiency, the CADD system is usually shared by several projects and is thus sometimes working on the project and sometimes off-stream working on another project. This functional relationship is shown in Figure 7.3.

This figure very simply segments the total required CADD time on

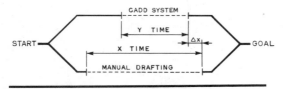

Figure 7.2 Matching the project efforts.

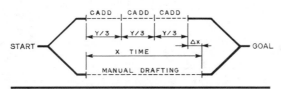

Figure 7.3 Intermittent project efforts.

project, y time, into three equal parts for demonstration purposes (although the actual functional time groups will be of varying lengths and certainly more than the merely three portions shown). Note that at the terminal condition of the project, the last CADD segment still occurs some Δx ahead of the final manual drafting effort.

What is not CADD

There is very little that cannot be handled by CADD. Most design and drafting functions can be and are being done by computer—but not by everybody with a CADD system and normally not all at once. A list of what is normally done on a CADD system and what is normally not done with CADD but handled manually is shown in Figure 7.4. Such a list is probably not absolutely true for any firm; every CADD practitioner will move items from one column to the other to suit the particular operation. In fact, the experienced CADD user will even apply CADD and manual methods differently on different projects.

Figure 7.4 does not attempt to list all possible types of documents nor to imply that CADD can only do some work or that manual methods must be used for other efforts. What is implied is that often the first use, or first continued use, of CADD will be for those items in the left-

Functions typically done by CADD (repligraphically)	Functions typically not done* by CADD (manually)
Basic plan modules	Complete floor plans
Site footprints	Forging blank configurations
Preliminary plans	Elevations
Spatial blocking diagrams	Single-line flow diagrams
Phased developments	Tooling standard limits
Adjacency layouts	Material flow patterns
Standard details	Primary sections
Three-dimensional and perspective views	Perspective views
"Intelligent drawing" databases	Site-work cut and fill
Areas and materials reports	Miscellaneous schedules
Orthographic views	Isometric views
General notes	Process flow diagrams
Critical path charts	Electrical schematics
	Electrical line tabs
	Piping and instrument diagrams
	Project title page
	Special-condition details

* CADD is capable of doing these, but they are not always assigned to CADD.

Figure 7.4 What is generally CADD and not CADD.

hand, repligraphic column. Likewise, those items found in the manual, right-hand column are often the last to be addressed by CADD.

Just to make matters interesting, Figure 7.4 also shows that perspective views are typically both done by CADD and not done by CADD. Also, the list includes "standard details" done by CADD but "special-condition details" typically done (at the last minute) manually. Further, after having gone through the hassles of manually doing electrical schematics and piping and instrumentation diagram (P&ID) drawings, one wonders why anyone would still do them without CADD.

7.2   Mixing CADD with Conventional Drafting

Because the plotted hardcopy functions of a CADD system are so much faster than manual methods, there is a tendency toward quickly plotting the image again, for any minor revisions, rather than resorting to manual drafting measures to clarify the situation. This speed of production by CADD is excellent but may lead to a mindset which quickly runs up massive expenses for plotter media and printed formats.

This situation is diagrammed in Figure 7.5. A drawing is initiated on the CADD system, thus creating a database. A hardcopy plot is then generated for offline reproduction and issuance for review and comment. All revisions are done strictly on the CADD system, thus maintaining a current database for the drawings. Subsequently, another hardcopy plot is created and replicated for comments. This sequence, generating numerous plots, continues for the life of the project.

Backtract a moment to Figure 5.9 and the accompanying text discussion in Chapter 5 of the alternatives to plotting on printed formats. Figure 5.9 provides several methods for substituting simple diazo reproductions for expensive printed formats, while implying that only the content of the drawings would be plotted. The myriad plots discussed in Figure 7.5 would either aggravate the situation of eating printed formats or would continue to take extra plot time to generate the drawing format as well as the drawing contents.

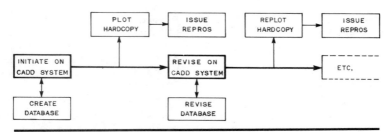

Figure 7.5 Continued, rapid replotting.

Drawing format control and specifically the limits of plotted area are critical to alternate format usage. If the typical outer limit of the CADD plot window is the format borderline rather than the outer, trim edge of a particular sheet, many of the alternate systems will be precluded. Similarly, some of the smaller vector plotters severely limit the maximum plotted area available.[B14]

Include manual convenience

When mixing CADD and manual drafting, care can be exercised both to work on the hardcopy plots for minor revisions and to maintain the database by reflecting those revisions. Figure 7.6 shows the functional path for creating drawings from a CADD database, generating hardcopy plots, and then making manual offline revisions to the hardcopy. The dotted line indicates that these revisions are also provided directly back to the CADD operator for inclusion into the database. However, a new hardcopy plot is not generated for each new revision.

Rather, the hardcopy plot with its manual revisions continues to accumulate further revisions through several review sessions. These subsequent revisions are also included in the CADD database. When the amount or extent of the revisions to the document reaches a given level, a new plot can be generated.

Under these conditions, the time required to configure a plot file, or plot spool, and then to de-spool or dump the file to the plotter is limited to only those occasions when it is truly productive. Further, the particular CADD project document or documents need not be continually accessed, thus leaving the CADD systems available for productive work on another project or another segment of the current project.

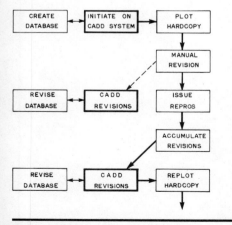

Figure 7.6 Occasional, rapid replotting.

Cutting out plotted details

The concept of using the CADD system where it is most productive is certainly not new; actually, that is the goal of CADD. It may not be most productive to be using the interactive graphic CADD system to constantly regenerate the same or similar images. This is especially true for construction and fabrication details.

Using the CADD system as a definitive and accurate drafting and filing system in terms of details and subsystems can be very productive and also a potential waste of valuable workstation and plotter time. Libraries of details and common symbols can be accurately, easily, and quickly drawn electronically. They can be cataloged, recalled, revised and reformatted, or rearranged to suit the many project needs.

One nice thing about the CADD systems is that once something is drawn, it need not be redrawn and is forever reusable (provided that it is not erased or written over). There is no need to recall, reconfigure, and replot a detail sheet for each project *unless the detail database is substantially changed.* Once plotted from the CADD system, the sets of details can be copied offline and reused for subsequent similar sheets. The detail's database need not be reaccessed unless the detail or subsystem needs to be substantially changed.

Figure 7.7 shows this synergistic repligraphic endeavor for a detail sheet. The selected details or subsystems are formatted and plotted for the first specific project (A). This quality plot is then contact-copied onto diazo or silver emulsion clear film or is simply photo-projection-restored onto a clear (not matte) film positive with or without the original title block and border. The individual details can then be cut out and redistributed, still offline, as required for the detail sheets of projects B and C. These clear films of the details are taped onto the formats of the new projects, and then the taped assemblies are photographically or electrostatically restored to produce new, workable originals.

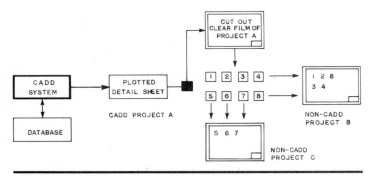

Figure 7.7 Reusing plotted details.

Revisions or additions to these previously plotted details usually are singular in nature: they apply to only one or two details. Only the affected details need be revised in the database. They can then be plotted, along with any new or additional details replicated onto clear film, and used to replace or augment the previous sets.

With this method there is no need to replot the entire detail sheet or the entire set of details. Further, the clear film copies of the quasi-standard details of subsystems can be untaped from the carrier sheets and filed for future use. In this manner, the CADD system is used to its best advantage: precision drafting (plotting) and easily recallable and revisable master filing, with an offline hardcopy database.

Photodrafting plus CADD

The vast number of image points, or pixels, required to faithfully capture all the gray tones in a photograph is beyond the practical memory and processing capability of current micro- and mini-CADD systems.[A48] Although the technology is in place and is being used in combining aerial photography and cartography,[A38] practical application at the micro-CADD level is not available except for the integration of manual photodrafting systems.

Follow the sequence of events shown in Figure 7.8. First a photograph is made of the object or area. (For purposes of this discussion, the photographs will be considered black and white; color photographic images prohibitively compound the data-handling problems.) The photograph or photographs are then combined with the drawing format by reprographic methods[A42, B7] to create a workable polyester clear or matte film "original" with the halftone photographs at some convenient size.

Selected reference points in the photographs are isolated, and three or more reference graphic arts targets or fiducials are added to the composite film original. This photodrawing is then taped to a digitizer board. The reference points and targets on the photographs are digitized into the CADD database. Other key portions of the photographic images can then be digitally entered. With this background data input from the photographs and targets, the CADD system can then be used to create the necessary additional images and text elements *on separate layers.*

Figure 7.9 continues this process, but now as output from the CADD system. By selectively shutting off layers within the CADD drawing, discrete plots can be made which would include the digitized target references and the CADD-added clarifying lines and text. These plots, which are the same size and on the same scale as the original photographic background drawing, can then be overlaid and visually aligned with the original photodrawing, using the targets as reference. Additionally, the selected reference points digitized from within the photos can be checked for alignment.

Since it is assumed that the complete photograph was not integrated into the CADD, it would be expected that some of the CADD-added imagery may have to be repositioned to work better with the photographs. This would mean reentering the CADD system, recalling the drawing, and relocating the images before again creating a new same-size plot with the reference targets. These plots are again aligned with the photographs and checked for convergence. Caution: Minor discrepancies in visual alignment may be caused by plot media slippage, which is dependent upon the plotting speed, resolution, and accuracy of the plotter.

At the last functional point in Figure 7.9, the layers of the targeted photodrawing and the matching, targeted CADD plot can be composited onto diazo or silver film using a contact vacuum frame. With a little forethought and some care in handling, the above-mentioned digitizing of targets and the input to CADD mentioned in Figure 7.8 can be done

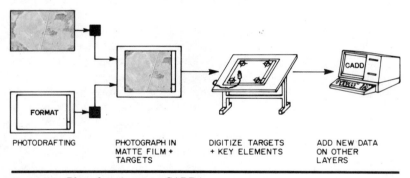

| PHOTODRAFTING | PHOTOGRAPH IN MATTE FILM + TARGETS | DIGITIZE TARGETS + KEY ELEMENTS | ADD NEW DATA ON OTHER LAYERS |

Figure 7.8 Photodata input to CADD.

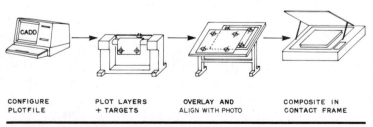

| CONFIGURE PLOTFILE | PLOT LAYERS + TARGETS | OVERLAY AND ALIGN WITH PHOTO | COMPOSITE IN CONTACT FRAME |

Figure 7.9 Photodata output from CADD.

before the photographs and the drawing formats are photographically composited. In this manner, the targeted CADD plots can be first checked for alignment with the photographs, and then photographically combined with the original photographs and formats to create a single, possibly variable-size, composite of all elements.

7.3 Mixing CADD with Pin-Registered Overlays

Ever-increasing emphasis is being directed toward as direct as possible a mixing of the CADD systems, with their increased throughput, with the advanced manual drafting techniques. This mixing is valid for in-house operations and for interfacing with outside consultants who are members of the project team but who may not have a compatible (nor any) CADD system. A great deal of this mixing of systems is done with layers and pin-registered overlay drafting.

In-house efforts

As discussed in Chapter 3, the CADD system is frequently used only for selected portions of a project. For example, preliminary design and development may use the CADD system most effectively, but then the actual working drawings may be completed by hand. The CADD system, in this instance, is used to generate the primary system schematics, P&ID's, site plans, and floor plans in workable hardcopy form. This establishes the basis for precision drafting and offline, offstream manual maintenance, while freeing the CADD system for work on other projects.

Figure 7.10 charts the multiple use of a CADD system for several projects. The left-hand flow path utilizes the CADD system through design and then creates registered hardcopy plots for manual completion. The right-hand flow path is first of all allowed to happen because the CADD system workstation has been released from its duties on project A. The project B path shows the (presently) much rarer form of project drawing production in which the CADD system is totally used for design and drafting. CADD is here used throughout the project, with ultimate plotting of the complete set of drawings. Project filing is a fully integrated software and hardware system.

Establishing registration

For the offline case in Figure 7.10, the issuance of *registered plots* may imply that the CADD hardcopies were made either on a flatbed plotter using pin-registered punch polyester film and a taped-in-place pinbar, or it may imply that the plotted images have included visual alignment targets or fiducials to allow for post-punching. Figure 7.11 isolates these two different hardcopy output functions. Note: The simple cylinder (drum) with grit-wheel plotters and the belted vector plotters cause the plot media to traverse a curve which would not accommodate the installation of a pinbar.

For those CADD workstations that include precision flatbed plotters, pin-registered plots can be achieved merely by using punched, 4-mil polyester matte film and the pinbar. The plotter then does the "drafting" directly upon registered layers. Each layer is electromagnetically registered within the CADD system, and the physical pins-and-holes offline registration will maintain that integrity.

For example, with a pinbar taped to the working surface of a flatbed

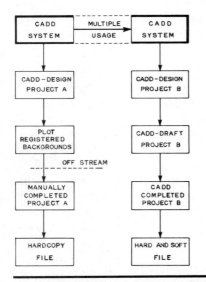

Figure 7.10 Partial and full use of CADD.

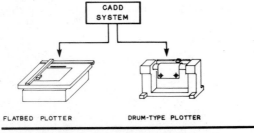

FLATBED PLOTTER   DRUM-TYPE PLOTTER

Figure 7.11 Flatbed or post-punched.

plotter, a precision-punched sheet of 4-mil polyester drafting film (matte on one side) is set on the alignment pins and corner-taped to the flatbed. The plotter head is positioned over the predetermined zero point (outside the drawing zone), and the command is given to plot only the specific background layer or the composite of layers required by each discipline or offline consultant.[A29]

Care must be taken to precisely zero the plotter head to a predetermined zero point on the flatbed board surface using the optical reticle provided with the plotters. This point is normally outside the plot image area, or at least at the lower left-hand corner of the image—comparable to the CADD database (0.00 X, 0.00 Y) zero point or the unique plot-window zero point. If the plotter head is precisely "zeroed," the head should always start in the same place, thus registering subsequent single- and multiple-layer composite plots.

Flatbed plotter head travel may require stricter control to avoid vectoring over or into the pinbar space. At the terminus of each plotted data layer, the plotter head can be subrouted to reposition over the zero point while a new layer of pin-registered 4-mil polyester drafting film replaces the finished plotted sheet.[A29]

For the drum-type and belt-bed plotters shown in Figure 7.11, where mechanical alignment with pins and precision-punched holes is not possible, visual alignment with targets or fiducials becomes the necessary alternative. These alignment points (a minimum of three located in opposite corners is required) will allow visual alignment on the punch frame for punching after plotting. It is indeed interesting that users of the high-precision instrument CADD rely upon the less precise visual alignment with targets for the bulk of their registered output, while advanced manual drafters rely upon the very precise pinbar with mechanical registration.

Initiated as a special symbol or layer applied to each drawing format in the CADD system, the three or four fiducials can be plotted as a separate set, at the final plot format size, on a sheet of 4-mil polyester film. This registered plot is then set on the punch frame, taped in place, and punched. Subsequent layers, each including the fiducial's "symbol layer," are plotted on 4-mil polyester matte film. They can then be visually aligned with the preset target template already on the punch frame and precision post-plot-punched.[A44]

Figure 7.12 defines the recommended locations for the four targets used by CADD systems to allow for offline registration via post-punching. Typically, the first target to be generated would be in the upper right corner. The horizontal bar of the target should line up with the top-edge borderline; the vertical bar of the target should be one-half the distance from the right-edge borderline to the trim edge of the sheet,

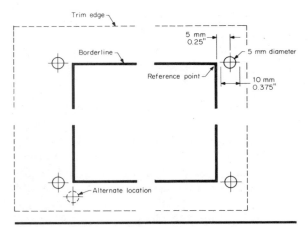

Figure 7.12 Targets for post-punching.

or 5 millimeters (0.25 inch), whichever is less. The target circle should have a 5-millimeter (0.25-inch) diameter and the cross bars should be 10 millimeters (0.375 inch) long and centered on the target circle.

This standard target can then be "unloaded," "copied," or made into a CADD "symbol" with the corner of the borderline as its reference point. This target symbol or "block element" can then be loaded or copied back onto the CADD layer at each of the remaining borderline corners as shown. Note that the centerline of the lower-right-hand corner target lines up with the bottom-edge borderline, as does the lower-left-hand target. Similarly, the upper-left-hand target is "mirrored" into position in line with the top-edge borderline.

These target positions allow for visual alignment, away from the body of the punch itself, and control in post-punching. The targets should be on their own discrete layer—possibly also with the dotted trim edgeline for reference—to allow subsequent combination with any other layer or group of layers.[A45, A46]

For those companies using the pin graphics audit block[B7] in the lower-left-hand corner of the binding edge of a drawing, this target position would cause an upward shifting of the audit block by a mere 10 to 12.5 millimeters (0.375 inch). As an alternate, this lower-left-hand target position could be moved down and to the right to align with the left-hand vertical border and below the bottom-edge borderline.

These offline registered layers would be handled just as if they were on a standard pin graphics project. However, with CADD assistance, major design scope changes could be implemented at the CADD workstation and then again register-plotted for offline completion.

Including the outside consultants

Figure 7.13 delineates the condition in which the production design project is initiated on the in-house CADD workstation with direct connection, or indirect connection via floppys, to outside consultants who have compatible CADD software and hardware systems. Unfortunately, the normal case is that the outside consultant or project team member often does not have a compatible CADD system, or is a non-CADD professional organization.

As document production efforts swing from the project's initiating discipline to the various consultants, the more difficult coordination of design communication and revision process becomes apparent. Since pin graphics with pin-registered polyester film layers greatly facilitates the sharing of data, CADD hardcopy output to the offline consultants should be issued as plots directly on pin-registered layers, using the methods described above.[A44]

These registered plots can then be duplicated onto several pin-registered clear-film sepia "slicks" for manual use by the various members of the design team. With the shared CADD background layers downloaded to pin-registered plots, the consultant's design documents are then created by the various offline disciplines as shared or specific and unique layers to the commmon plot bases. By maintaining registration offline, later revisions at the originating CADD database level can be again transmitted by registered plots out to the consultants.

In the typical case, the various outside consultants need apply only one pin-registered layer over the initiating discipline's plotted base in order to communicate their portion of the design. Special multiple-use consultant bases can also be created as required. Some consultants' drawings, such as detail sheets and some piping (P&ID) and schematic diagrams not requiring pin graphics, are considered off-system and are not affected unless certain elements of these sections and details are or can be shared from the CADD database.

CADD-plotted layers or segments of the design can of course be

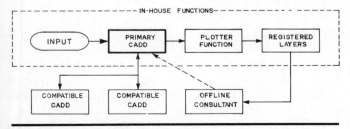

Figure 7.13 Offline consultants.

copied by repligraphic techniques onto a variety of mediums as required for renderings, separate submittals, special filings, etc. In addition, design portions and alternate design schemes created outside the CADD pin graphics system can be digitized into the database for later registered or nonregistered plotted hardcopy output. Consideration should be given to the erasability and workability of these off-system copies.

Plot jam

As discussed in previous chapters, all the drawings created using the advanced design and drafting tool CADD must be transferred to plot file and then physically plotted onto a medium suitable for further reproduction or display. Even with the very rapid plotter systems and techniques available, quite often a large number of drawings in the plot file await access to the plotter. This backlog, or "plot jam," can quickly pile up to staggering proportions.[A29]

For example, 100 drawings with an average plot time of 30 minutes each will require 3000 plot-minutes or 50 plot-hours of actual plot run time (not including maintenance and medium loading and unloading time). This would mean 2½ days of round-the-clock production plotting or 5 plot-days at 10 hours per day, with no time left over for other necessary checkplots. The alternatives are to invest in an electrostatic plotter, to use an outside service bureau, or to otherwise directly reduce the vector plot time.

Figure 7.14 delineates the normal sequence for CADD output to plotted hardcopy via the plot file. The four drawings shown are considered to have average image density and to be on A1 (D) size sheets. Each drawing in this set is made up of four to five representative layers of common plus unique information. It should be noted that the normal CADD drawing could be considered as having anywhere from 5 to 20 layers. To reduce overall plot time, these A1 (D) size sheets all have preprinted title block and border formats.

After the plots have been completed, including all replotting necessary to correct output errors, the hardcopy originals then must be contact-diazo-copied, electrostatically, micrographically or photographically re-stored, and reproduced for project distribution and filing.

The average plot times for each of the four drawings shown in Figure 7.14 are charted in Figure 7.15. Each sheet has its total plot time as well as the respective plot-minutes for each layer (as if they were separately isolated). As these layers are shared, their respective plot times are incorporated into the total. Total actual plot time accumulates to 132 plot-minutes for these four drawings. The grand total time for production plot output of all drawings requires adding an additional 10 to 20 percent of plot time to the total for plot media and materials handling.[A29]

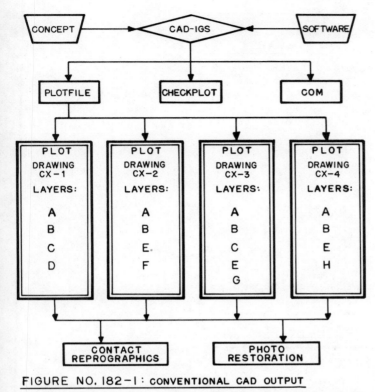

FIGURE NO. 182–1: CONVENTIONAL CAD OUTPUT

Figure 7.14 Conventional CADD output.

Plot flow

Advanced drafting systems, including repligraphic drafting, have several similar rules:

- Don't draw the same line twice.
- Don't file the same layer twice.
- Don't plot the same layer twice.

Using this logic, consider that the layers shown in Figure 7.14 were actually accessed as separate-layer functions in the CADD system and therefore it would be not only more logical but also more practical to plot this data in separate layers. Refer also to Figure 6.3.

Figure 7.16 delineates the CADD output as separate pin-registered, polyester, 4-mil drafting film layers. As mentioned previously concerning Figure 7.12, these registered layers could be from a flatbed plotter using a pinbar and punched film, or from a drum-type or belt-bed plotter using

CONVENTIONAL PLOT TIMES CHART			
DRAWING NO.	DATA LAYER	LAYER TIME	DRAWING TIME
CX – 1	A B C D	5 8 8 9	30
CX – 2	A B E F	5 8 11 9	33
CX – 3	A B C E G	5 8 8 11 7	39
CX – 4	A B E H	5 8 11 6	30
TOTAL 4 DRAWINGS		132 MINUTES	

FIGURE NO. 182–1A: PLOT JAM

Figure 7.15 Plot jam.

plotted targets or registration fiducials. Multiple data layers can be programmed for plotting together on a single registered sheet or on separate sheets, depending upon how the plot file is loaded.[A29]

After plotting, and post-punching if necessary, these layers can be again composited with contact diazo methods or large-format electrostatic, or they can be restored via process photonegatives onto wash-off polyester film positives. Current state of the art in repligraphics also allows some sidestepping of this lengthy full-size plotting by generating pin-registered composite or layered negatives, at convenient reduced sizes, using laser imaging techniques. Refer to Chapter 5.

Figure 7.17 charts this alternate output function as a total of the individual layers. Not plotting the same layer twice, or even more times, causes the net plot time to drop from 132 to 63 plot-minutes for this example. The absence of redundant replotting times is the key, even though an additional 10 to 20 percent for media handling must still be added. The original four hardcopy plots on printed formats thus become eight registered layer plots on blank, nonbordered, 4-mil polyester matte film. The printed format need only be borrowed for a short time to incorporate its image into the contact composites and photocomposites.

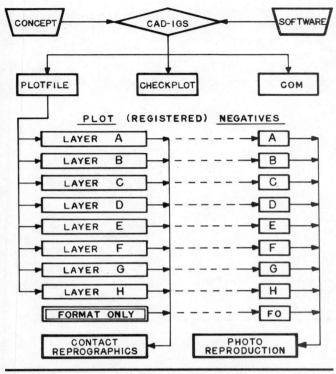

Figure 7.16 CADD output to pin graphics.

Using these pin-registered or pin graphics layering techniques, the original plot-jam example of 100 plotted drawings requiring 3000 plot-minutes could now be done in approximately 2250 plot-minutes.

The full set of plots may not be affected by this layering function. If only 50 percent of the drawings are done with registered layers, which would save 50 percent of their total plot-minutes, then the remaining half of the plots would take 1500 plot-minutes and the layered set would require only 750 plot-minutes—thus developing the net 2250 plot-minutes noted. This productivity increase would net at least a 25 percent savings in plot time and operator expense. This savings would be far more than the cost of the additional repligraphics and reprographics labor and materials.

Differentiated layers

Unless CADD hardcopy output is done with multicolors, the typical image is monochrome, with black lines on a white field. All too often this plotted output does not have any substantial differentiation of line weight for lines and text.

PIN GRAPHICS	
PLOT TIMES CHART	
DATA LAYER	PLOT TIME
A	5
B	8
C	8
D	9
E	11
F	9
G	7
H	6
TOTAL 8 SHEETS (4 COMPOSITES)	63 MINUTES

Figure 7.17 Plot flow.

As discussed in Chapter 5, the CADD software should be capable of reconfiguration to set certain line weights, with logical pens and with colors for selected layers or image elements. If the plotter used in Figure 7.14 to create the four drawings were set up such that at least two pen sizes, a 00 (0.30 millimenter) and a 1 (0.50 millimeter) or 2 (.60 millimeter), were set in the penholder, the common layers could be plotted with the thinner lines while the unique discipline layers could be plotted with more boldness, using the twice-as-thick pen size.

However, this pen differentiation, or even multistroking for wide images, does not achieve the clarity of drawing communication that is shown in Figure 4.14. For all practical purposes, based upon data element handling and system file space, screen tinting for subdued imaging cannot be directly addressed by CADD systems. Yet the mixing of CADD output with the human-cadd layered drafting, manual methods can in fact achieve this most productive image differentiation.

Figure 7.18 collects the concepts of practical computer interaction, using the design and drafting tools of CADD software and hardware, and incorporates the advanced drafting methods of pin-registered overlays. Although the CADD system configuration and input methods are very important, it is the output from the system which is utilized to create, construct, fabricate, or renovate the original concept into usable form.

In this case, the normal CADD plot generates four sheets (C-1, C-2, C-3, and C-4) as composite images from database layers, but these layers need to be replotted. For superior image differentiation, the plots should be in colors which match the displayed imagery. Proper selection of those plot colors (i.e., green fades out partially while blue fades out too much), along with multistroking or other line-width controls, will

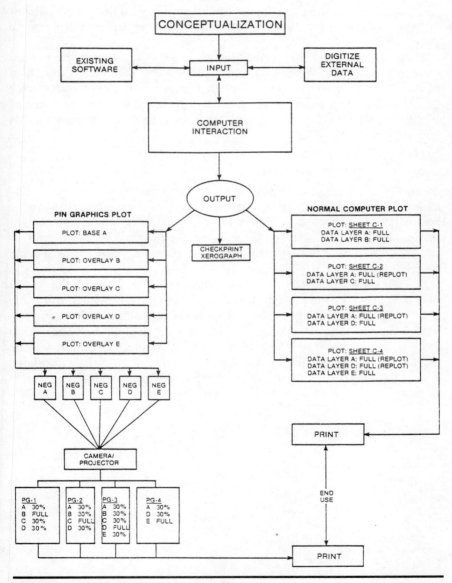

Figure 7.18 Useful end-use imagery.

help to achieve some discipline separation. But if the output is only monochrome and monoline, then the communication potential will be lost unless hardcopy layer separation is used.

The left-hand side of Figure 7.18 follows the pin graphics plot logic through the creation of full-size registered layers or laser-imaged and registered A4 (A) size negatives culminating in four composites. These four composite drawings (PG-1, PG-2, PG-3, and PG-4) include the notations for subduing the image of certain layers down to 30 percent of their respective gray scale, whole allowing selected layers to remain full strength.

However, the "end-use" condition for the results of both the normal computer plot and the pin graphics plot is the distributed and filed print. *Note: A true test for any plotted image is not that image itself but rather the first reproduction from that image.* Thus, the bottom line of the use of CADD systems must still be considered in terms of its hardcopy output.

Considering the end result first

In the transition from conventional drafting to the use of computer-aided design and drafting systems, the first requirements seem to be acquisition and training. From these descend the system management and maintenance functions. Only then is any consideration given to the real issue of software and hardware systems, *application* to specific project needs.

Once the CADD system is applied to a project or design task, it soon becomes very clear that it is the *output from CADD* which truly sets the configurations for how the system is to be used and thus properly establishes the acquisitional needs. Careful thought about how the CADD system will be used and how its end result (hardcopy) output will be used is necessary at the outset. These functions must be considered before an investment in this very effective repligraphic drafting system is made.

Glossary

access The act of selecting, enabling or recalling a device, file, or function using a specific address code or command.

address The coordinates or coding which provides specific identification for accessing data, devices, or functions.

algorithm The logic gate flow path for describing a function or process so that it can be accomplished by software programming.

aliasing The offsetting or stair-step appearance of a line on a raster display caused by the resolution or pixel count. See also *jaggies*.

alphanumeric The general term used to describe letters of the alphabet (alpha), punctuation elements, and numbers (numeric) as characters distinct from graphic lines and curves.

analog Dealing with data presentation in a continuous stream, as does a clock with a sweep hand; opposite to digital. See also *digital*.

antialiasing The incorporation of nearby pixels in the area of image offsets to smooth out jagged-edged images. Especially useful with colors.

aperture card A small card with a rectangular cutout specifically designed for mounting microfilm; may contain card-reader punched holes.

applications software Computer programs which perform specific functions and are applied to selected efforts (i.e., CADD or spreadsheet).

architecture A physical arrangement of functional elements in which the synergistic whole accomplishes a designated task; in computers, the physical layout of hardware.

archival quality The degree to which hardcopy or softcopy data will retain its integrity and characteristics during a period of use and storage.

ASCII code American Standard Code for Information Interchange binary coding (digital number) assigned to alphanumeric characters.

asynchronous Data transmission upon demand rather than in a set sequence.

attribute The characteristics associated with database elements: text font, line type, color, part number, weight, reference code, etc.

Autopositive An Eastman Kodak trade name for certain photographic direct positive intermediates.

background The nonimaged area of a display or plot or print; also, the common or shared information or layers in CADD and pin graphics.

backup A copy of the database or software which assures safe file continuity.

Basic Beginners' All-Purpose Symbolic Instruction Code, a general software programming tool with which applications software can be created.

batch processing Sequential, functional running of program sets of files requiring no interactive operator control.

baud Digital information transfer rate associated with modems and hardwire interchanges of data in bits per second.

binary A characterization of data as having only two states: 1 or 0, yes or no, on or off. This is the primary functional mode of computers.

bit A contraction of *binary* dig*it,* which as a binary has only the form of a 1 or a 0.

bit map A representation of the CRT display on which each resolution pixel is addressed by individual bits for enhanced graphic control.

blowback The act of projecting a photographic image. See also *projection image.*

blueline A dry-process diazo print with blue lines on a white background.

blueprint A wet-process negative image reproduction with white lines on a blue field; a generic copying term taken from a now-little-used process.

boot Initiating sequence for computer start-up or restart which generally clears RAM memory and resets primary input-output functions.

bps Bits per second; generally used to describe data transfer rates.

break A programmed key, menu field, or command which stops the operation of a program. See also *escape.*

buffer Short-term or frequently purged and refilled memory storage area for use in data transfer and batch processing.

bug A software problem or error.

bus An electronic connection between computer input-output devices.

byte An array of 8 binary digits, or bits.

CAD Computer-aided design or computer-aided drafting.

CADD Computer-aided design and drafting.

CAE Computer-aided engineering.

CAM Computer-aided manufacturing.

camera projector Process equipment of relatively large size which uses lenses to capture images as negatives and then to project them back (using the same lenses and internal light sources) at the same or varying sizes to create a positive copy. See also *blowback.*

cartridge   or cartridge disk   An electromagnetically coated circular, flat, metallic or vinyl platter encased in a hard plastic card and used for storing and retrieving computer data.

cassette   A small magnetic tape cartridge for program or data storage.

CAT   Computer-aided testing.

character   An alphanumeric unit of data normally described by 1 byte.

chip   A principal memory and control device consisting of microminiaturized electronic circuits on a small segment of semiconductor material.

circuit board   A complex array of electronic elements and memory chips.

CIM   Computer-integrated manufacturing.

clipping   The selection of specific graphic images with a hard boundary edge which cuts or clips discrete portions of an overall image.

clock   A time-cycle function which sets the pulse rate for computer operations.

Cobol   Common Business Oriented Language for computer programming.

code   Symbolic representation of software programming commands and data.

color   A phenomenon in which light gives differing polychromatic hues and tints; displayed with combinations of red, green, and blue projections.

color transparency   A slide; a film positive which portrays a subject in natural colors and is generally viewed by transmitted light.

COM   Computer output to microfilm as aperture cards, roll, or microfiche.

command   An operator instruction initiated by menu selection or keyboard which directs the functions of a computer.

compatibility   The ability of software and hardware sets to work together.

compiler   A software translator between language levels. See also *interpreter*.

composite   The combination of several registered layers into one whole. See also *overlay; underlay*.

computer system   All the hardware, software, and peripherals required to complete an input-output production set.

contact frame   A device used for making same-size reproductions from translucent materials held in immediate contact. Items in contact are exposed through a glass cover and held in position normally by vacuum. See also *vacuum frame*.

continuous tone   In a reproduction of a photograph, a varying gradation of gray densities between black and white. See also *halftone*.

contrast   Difference in tone between the darker and the lighter parts of an image.

controller   The sets of firmware which manage the handshake between the CPU and the peripheral displays, plotters, and other systems.

coordinates   The X-, Y-, and Z-axis reference numbers which are used to locate a graphic point within the database. See also *bit map*.

copy board   The portion of a process camera on which the object to be photographed (the art copy or the drawing or plot) is mounted.

CPM   Control Program for Microcomputer; an operating system developed by Digital Research.

CPU   Central processing unit; the set of circuit boards and computer chips which constitute the core or working area of a computer.

crash   A major malfunction within a computer system.

create   To generate lines and text in CADD.

cross hairs   Short or long reference lines on the display CRT the intersection of which represents the current operating position. See also *cursor.*

CRT   Cathode ray tube or display monitor; the primary visual output peripheral for the computer.

cursor   A single block of pixels, square or round dots, or cross hairs which define the current command or operating position. See also *cross hairs.*

cut and tape   A systems drafting method in which reusable data images are cut out from a copy, relocated, and then taped in place.

daisy wheel printer   A letter-quality printer which uses a circular element in conjunction with a strike hammer to form the letters, numbers, and symbols of alphanumeric data. See also *dot matrix printer; ink-jet printer; letter-quality printer.*

data   Reference information stored in computer memory as binary digit combinations in discrete files representing all graphic and alphanumeric elements and positions.

database   The complete set of data elements pertaining to a particular function, operation, or project; a selected accumulation of data.

data processing (DP)   Primarily devoted to the manipulation of numeric data. Compare with *word processing.*

DBMS   Database management system; complete control over all graphic and alphanumeric aspects of a system or facility by fully utilizing the stored data and its attributes.

debugging   Correcting, deleting, or revising the errors or problems in a computer program software or database.

design   The accumulation of all pertinent data and options for a specific situation and the resolution of the needs of that situation.

development   Conversion of an invisible latent photographic image into visible form by reducing sensitized silver halide to metallic silver; conversion of a partially exposed diazonium coating with ammonia vapor to produce a positive azo dye image.

diagnostic   Describing a prompt or report from the computer control program concerning an error condition or malfunction.

diazo process   A reproduction method using materials coated with a light-sensitive, colored diazonium salt that, after exposure, is developed with ammonia vapor.

digital Dealing with individual, mutually exclusive states.

digitize To translate an image or object into digital reference coordinates.

dimensional stability The relative ability of materials to maintain their size and shape.

dimensioning Designation of the distance between selected points with the use of reference lines, arrowheads, and appropriate nomenclature.

direct positive A reproduction copy made from a positive image, in which another positive image is formed without an intermediate negative.

direct print A positive reproduction on diazo-sensitized materials made directly from a translucent original.

disk An electromagnetically coated, circular, flat metallic platter used for storing and retrieving computer data. See also *softcopy*.

diskette Often referred to as "floppy disk"; an electromagnetically coated, circular, flat polyester platter used for storing and retrieving data.

disk drive A device for receiving, holding, and rotating data disks including an electromagnetic read-write head for retrieval and storage of the magnetic charges (information) on the disks.

display The visual output from a computer, represented as pixels of various brightness and color on the CRT monitor.

documentation A written hardcopy set of instructions, usually in notebook form, required for proper operation and maintenance of the computer software, hardware, and peripherals.

DOS Disk operating system; controls the functioning of a computer.

dot matrix printer A graphic printer which forms alphanumeric characters, lines, and curves with a very close array of dots which are controlled by the printer firmware and the computer software output. See also *daisy wheel printer; ink-jet printer; letter-quality printer.*

double density A disk recording method which compresses onto a disk vastly more than the usual amount of read-write data.

double-sided Electromagnetically coated, formatted, and used on both sides (of a disk), for maximum data storage and utilization.

downtime A period when a system or device is not functioning.

dragging Moving a cursor or graphic element across the display.

draw To generate a graphic element or text string using command sequences and cursor control.

duplicate An intermediate copy used to replace original drawings or data.

editor Control program which manages the processing of words and data.

EDP Electronic data processing. See *data processing.*

electronic drafting The generation of lines, curves, and text elements by defining their characteristics and coordinates in binary digit form within an electromagnetic medium.

electrostatic plotter A hardcopy output device which produces images in dot matrix form in a raster format using heat and graphite toner.

emulator A control program that allows differing computer systems to share data and software so as to generate the same images. See *compatibility*.

emulsion A single-layer or multilayer coating of gelatinous material over various substrates which carries photochemicals for exposure and development or acts as a drafting surface.

endpoint The last reference point on a graphic line or curve. See also *startpoint*.

enlargement Method for increasing image scale.

EPROM Erasable programmable read-only memory; a form of firmware that can be specifically erased and then reprogrammed.

error A diagnostic message displayed on a monitor in response to incorrect commands or data input.

escape (ESC) Generally a key, menu field, or command that resets interpretation of subsequent commands; may break the function of a current program activity. See also *break*.

execute An instruction to commence or start a program.

exposure The introduction of light for a predetermined period of time and with selected intensity.

fading Loss of density of an image.

file A collection of interrelated data.

film positive A positive reproduction made on film with a photographic emulsion.

firmware Software programming resident in ROM chips and EPROMS in the hardware.

fixed disk An electromagnetically coated high-density disk which is not removable from its compartment. See also *Winchester disk*.

fix line A photographic film image within an emulsion that requires a two-solution eradicator.

flag An attribute or status indicator which can be attached to data images, reference points, and text groups to allow selective recall.

floppy disk See *diskette*.

format The layout area or boundary line of artwork, drawings, and plots.

FORTRAN *For*mula *tran*slator; a standardized and interchangeable computer language for engineering work.

frame An individual picture in a strip of motion picture film, roll of microfilm, or portion of microfiche.

function key A typewriter keyboard key which has specific command attributes and which can often be reprogrammed.

generate To create or draw lines, curves, and text elements within a CADD database.

generation A reproduction from the original.

ghost A second or retained image that is not usually desired.

graphics Any drawn image, computer-generated display, or plotted image; can be construed to mean only straight lines and curves, with no alphanumeric text.

grid Intersecting lines, displayed as lines or intersection points only, which act as references or as limits to movement.

halftone In a reproduction of a photograph, gradation of tone which is conveyed by various-sized dots and white spaces using a variable-density screen. See also *continuous tone.*

hardcopy Printed, plotted, or photographed physical reproduction of a database; relatively more permanent than electromagnetic data. See also *softcopy.*

hard disk An electromagnetically coated, high-density disk which is generally double-sided and is often found in a stack of several disks; used for very large memory storage.

hardware The CPU, monitor, disks, plotter, and other physical components of a computer system. See also *software.*

hatching From "cross-hatching"; filling a defined area with a selected pattern of lines or other graphic elements. See also *in-fill.*

head The electronic element which traverses a disk or tape to read, write, or erase electromagnetic charges (the stored data).

help Technical support and backup prompts on how to use the software.

high-resolution Improved image quality in visual display and hardcopy output based upon increasing numbers of pixels, dots-per-inch, and general accuracy.

IC Integrated circuit; composed of numerous chips and interconnected electronic components.

ICON A command, function, or menu item represented as a graphic picture.

image A likeness which appears on a CRT display, a hardcopy plot, or a reproduced copy.

imaging Processing a graphics database to produce a computer display or plot.

in-fill Pattern generation within a defined boundary. See also *hatching.*

ink-jet printer A hardcopy output device which dispenses discrete droplets of ink in a high-resolution dot matrix raster fashion. See also *daisy wheel printer; dot matrix printer; ink-jet printer.*

input   Commands, data, and other information entered into the database or RAM.

instruction   A single logical or arithmatic command in a software program.

interactive   Describing communication between operator and computer in which input is followed by purposeful and fitting responses.

interactive display   A CRT monitor with an embedded wire-mesh grid for use with a touch-sensitive or probe-activated cursor for menu control.

interface   The linkage or intimate transition between elements or entities.

intermediate   A translucent reproduction from an original drawing, print, or plot which is used in place of the original for making direct copies.

interpreter   A software language translation function. See also *compiler.*

I/O   Input-output; usually designating a function or interface port.

jaggies   Apparent offsetting of displayed or plotted lines and curves caused by low resolution and raster effect. See also *aliasing.*

joystick   An input hardware component which serves to control the location of the cursor.

justification   Alignment function, may be left, center, right, or right and left.

K   Kilo; a factor of 1000, 1024 bytes of computer memory.

keyboard   A complete QWERTY-style typewriter key set, usually with additional numeric keys, cursor direction, and programmed function keys.

keypad   Usually the numeric keyboards of a hand-held computer.

laminated   Composed of two or more layers held in contact.

laser plotter   A hardcopy output device that uses rectified light amplification to expose photographic emulsions in vector or raster arrays.

layers   Physical or logical separations of component elements considered as two-dimensional planes stacked and registered in a third dimension. See also *overlay drafting; pin graphics.*

LCD   Liquid crystal display.

LED   Light-emitting diode.

letter-quality printer   A dot matrix or daisy wheel printer that produces alphanumeric characters equal to that of a typewriter. See also *daisy wheel printer; dot matrix printer; ink-jet printer.*

library   A set of graphic images, software programs, drawing files, or data.

light pen   A digital cursor control or input device that uses light-sensitive diode sets for interface and control.

line copy   An original or graphic image containing only lines and solid fields with no intermediate tones; can include text.

line negative   A high-contrast negative image that incorporates only black or white (clear) images; does not include continuous tone.

line type Functional and logical attributes and display image characteristics of generated graphic images.

lithography A printing process in which the image to be printed is ink-receptive and the blank area is ink-repellent; useful for high-quality, high-volume printing in monchrome and color. See also *offset printing.*

load The program function of setting file data into a register for processing.

logic The control sequence for functioning; as in the logic board of the CPU.

loop The process step of sequencing through a program or file and then returning to the start of that register for a recycle or data feedback.

M Mega; a factor of 1 million; for computers 1,048,576 bytes of data.

machine code A fundamental, binary control instruction language for computers.

macro An operator-defined, high-level language control program.

magnetic tape Electromagnetically coated polyester film mounted on reels; used for mass storage and backup of database and software.

mainframe A relatively large CPU and computer hardware set. See also *macro-computer; minicomputer.*

masking Using opaque material to cut off exposures to certain areas of graphic images and reproductions to produce desired effects.

mass storage Softcopy media for storage of vast amounts of data. See also *hard disk; magnetic tape.*

master An original from which reproductions are made. See also *original.*

matrix A coordinate set of X-, Y-, and Z-axis references.

matte Drafting surface on polyester films; a dull, glossfree surface finish.

memory Primary data handling and storage function and location; increase in memory is usually related to increase in processing speed.

menu A formatted area with icons, abbreviated command names, and macro functions which can be selected as program options.

menu-driven Describing a computer system which accepts commands from cursor-selected or probe-selected menu items.

merge Integration or mixing of two or more compatible programs or data files.

microcomputer A physically small computer system with limited memory, comparatively few hardware elements, and generally slow processing speed. See also *mainframe; minicomputer.*

microfiche Film that is 105 millimeters wide and contains microimages in a group pattern.

microfilm Fine-grain, high-resolution film containing an image greatly reduced in size from the original.

microprocessor A primary control or function chip in the CPU of a micro-computer system; often found in combinations of chips.

minicomputer A computer that is physically larger and more powerful than a microcomputer system, and that has numerous microprocessors but is much smaller than a mainframe. See also *mainframe; microcomputer.*

mirror A reverse-image function with right-left or top-down flip.

mnemonics Alphanumeric abbreviations of commands, functions, and macros to shorten command keystrokes and to save menu space.

modem Modulator-demodulator; converts binary data signals into and from high-frequency telecommunication signals.

monitor CRT display hardware.

mouse A cursor control device with function keys requiring movement by hand over a flat surface. See also *puck.*

multiprocessing Describing a computer system that utilizes several micro-processor chips.

Mylar A Dupont Company trade name for a polyester-type film of high strength and dimensional stability, which is used as a base stock for light-sensitive photographic coatings and drafting films.

NC Numerical control uses X, Y, and Z reference coordinates with tool path instructions for computer control of machine tool equipment.

negative A black background with white or clear images on photographic film or paper; can be in any of several different sizes.

negative chase The area of a process camera or a camera projector on which a negative is mounted for exposure or blowback.

network Hard-wired or telecommunication-linked compatible computer sys-tems; may share database or software programs.

nonreproducible Not intended for use as an intermediate master or second original; generally opaque; often blue or light violet in color.

number crunching High-volume processing of arithmetic data.

numeric pad A keypad which includes numbers only (no alphabetic characters).

offline Separate or disconnected from the computer system.

offset printing Indirect photolithography in which an image is transferred to a blanket or cylinder which in turn transfers the image to a copy medium. See also *lithography.*

online Connected to or integrated with a computer system.

opacity Nontranslucency; the property of a medium which prevents dark objects on or in contact with the back of the medium from being seen through the medium.

opaque copy Material which is impervious to light.

opaquing Working on an original or negative to block out selected images.

operating system   Primary computer control system software and firmware.

original   Material or database from which images are made. See also *master*.

origin point   Coordinate reference system simultaneous-zero location for X, Y, and Z axes. See also *zero point*.

orthochromatic   Describing photographic material that is sensitive to ultraviolet, blue, and green light and that reproduces red as black.

orthographic projection   Two-dimensional representation of a three-dimensional object using at least three mutually perpendicular views.

output   Response from input command and result from software processing; usually displayed on the monitor or generated as hardcopy or softcopy.

overlay   An interrelated and registered layer used to form a composite. See also *composite; underlay*.

overlay drafting   Separation of common data images onto several layers of registered drafting film (not paper) to allow multiple use of those images. See also *layers; pin graphics*.

paging   Switching between data blocks.

panning   Scrolling or lateral movement of displayed image.

panchromatic   Describing photographic film that is sensitive to ultraviolet light and all colors of the visible spectrum; reproduces all colors in their approximate tone values of gray.

parallax   Apparent change in shape of object as a function of viewing angle.

Pascal   A high-level software language for general programming.

password   A security procedure using alphanumeric character strings for access control.

pasteup   A composite drawing produced by pasting or taping individual segments onto a format or carrier sheet before reproduction.

peripheral   An interconnected input-output hardware device such as a monitor, disk drive, modem, or plotter.

perspective   Use of vanishing points to approximate the three-dimensional relationships of depth, height, and width on a two-dimensional plane.

photodrafting   Combining sections of several drawings and photographs into a single composite on drafting film using process-photographic techniques.

pinbar   A strip of stainless spring steel with precisely set pins; used for overlay registration alignment.

pin graphics   Precise mechanical alignment of separate film overlays by means of punched holes and a pinbar. See also *layers; overlay drafting*.

pixel   A single point on a raster display; an increased number of pixels in a set area increases resolution.

plotter   A hardcopy device that uses electrostatic, ink-jet, or photographic devices, a laser, or pens to generate a graphic image by computer control.

polar coordinates   Reference locations utilizing distance and angular direction.

polyester film   See *Mylar*.

polygon fill   See *in-fill* and *hatching*.

positive   Generally a white backgrond with black, gray-toned, or colored images; a normal-reading print from any type of negative or in the diazo process from another positive or an original.

primary memory   See *RAM*.

primitives   Simplest forms of graphic and alphanumeric elements.

print   A positive-reading reproduction.

printed circuit   An electronic circuit produced from artwork by photographic, etching, or silk screen processes.

printer   An alphanumeric hardcopy-producing device usually not suitable for producing graphics.

print head   The image-forming device of a printer.

probe   A menu-activating or cursor control device.

projection image   A photographic image made through a lens; may be enlarged, reduced, or used same size. See also *blowback*.

process camera   Large-format photographic equipment including a copy board, lights, lenses, controls, and chases for creating multisize negatives and positives with very high precision.

processing   Treatment of exposed material to make a latent image visible.

processor   A computer control device. See also *microprocessor*.

program   A command sequence list in appropriate software language based upon logic sequence.

PROM   Programmable read-only memory; once established, the commands remain permanently set.

puck   A cursor control and digitizing device with function keys utilizing cross hairs for precise manual positioning. See also *mouse*.

quadrant   One quarter of a space.

RAM   Random access memory; a primary working memory which is readily programmable, temporary, dynamic, and volatile (can be erased if power is lost).

raster plotter   A hardcopy device which creates images as an array of dots.

raster scan   A display method using a regular series of dots to form an image and the background for that image.

reader-printer   A micrographic device which both displays a microfilm image and creates a projected hardcopy positive from that image.

real time   Simultaneous animation, computation, and display function.

reduction   A method of decreasing the size or scale of an image.

reduction-enlargement ratio The relative change or linear measurement between an original and a reduced or enlarged reproduction; usually stated in the form 0.20x, 0.65x, 5x, 18.5x, etc.

reflected light Light which falls on an object or image and then is projected back. See also *transmitted light*.

refresh To redraw or repaint a CRT display image continually (at a preset clock speed or rate) in order to maintain picture brightness.

register To load data into a buffer for processing.

registration Precise alignment, using targets or pinbars and punched holes of several overlay images. See also *layers; overlay drafting; pin graphics*.

reprodrafting Any combination of manual and machine or photoassisted drawing techniques.

reproducible Capable of producing copies.

repligraphics The handling of hardcopy output from CADD systems.

reprographics The art and science of reproducing documents.

resolution The ability to render visible fine detail; a measure of sharpness.

restoration The process of improving existing document and database images.

return Command instruction to end current sequence and reset to previous instruction set.

reverse image An image in which alphanumeric characters and graphics appear backward (except when viewed through the back of the medium); or black characters on a white screen display where white on black is standard. See also *right image*.

RGB Red, green, and blue; the three principal display colors for polychromatic monitors and color hardcopy output devices.

right image An image in which text and graphics are readable from front or side. See also *reverse image*.

ROM Read-only memory; memory that is not reprogrammable and is not usually affected by power loss.

rotation Revolving of a graphic or text element around a selected reference point.

scale Relative size of a drawing image as compared with the actual object.

scale factor See *reduction-enlargement ratio*.

screen A CRT display monitor face.

screen tint Reduction of an image to a series of dots and open spaces so as to create a copy of that image in tones of gray.

scribing A drawing process in which a stylus is used to cut lines in a suitably prepared stock; generally used for mapping.

scrolling   Vertical movement of display images (up or down) to permit further display. See also *panning*.

sector   A defined segment of disk (memory) space or magnetic tape section.

semiconductor   A doped coating which has an electromagnetic potential between that of a true conductor and that of a true insulator; one principle behind computer chips and microprocessors.

sensitized   Coated with an emulsion sensitive to light.

sensor   A device which translates and transmits an analog signal to a digital processor.

sepia   Diazo materials with reddish-brown line imagery.

sequential access   Data acquisition in a set order.

shelf life   Period of time before deterioration renders sensitized materials unsuitable for their primary function.

silver halide   A light-sensitive silver compound or salt such as silver bromide, silver chloride, or silver iodide used for photographic emulsions.

single density   Standard recording rate or capability of diskettes.

single-sided   Describing diskette with only one side coated or available for data storage or recording.

softcopy   See also *disk; hardcopy.*

software   The instructions, commands, and necessary electronic memory required to operate and control a computer; the programming. See also *hardware*.

sort   To define or register items in a set order.

source language   Fundamental software coding.

stand-alone   Having the software and hardware capability to operate independently.

stair-stepping   See *aliasing; jaggies.*

start-point   The initial reference coordinate of a line, a curve, or a primitive. See also *end-point.*

static memory   ROM and other memory which is left intact after power loss.

stick-on   An adhesive-backed decal material, clear or opaque, which has received a copy image and which is then applied to an original.

stripping   The alignment and cutting, then taping, of negatives and artwork for final reproduction.

system   An interrelated, interconnected, and often synergistic set of software programs and hardware equipment designed or arranged for a purpose.

tablet   A flat surface underlaid with a very fine grid of wires which work with a probe or puck for menu selection, cursor control, or digitizing.

tape   An electromagnetically coated polyester recording medium.

telecommunications   Interconnections of data via telephone systems.

telephone modem See *modem.*

terminal An input device such as a keyboard and an output device such as a monitor, printer, or plotter.

text Individual and sets of alphanumeric characters which may have varying attributes; distinct from graphic lines and curves. See also *attributes.*

throughput The amount of data processed in a portion of time or by a selected function.

thumb-wheels Cursor control devices.

time-sharing Sharing of database or CPU functions, usually leased or rented.

trace The electron beam path on a display monitor which results in an image.

tracing Drawing over an existing image usually onto a translucent layer or with a digitizer puck.

track Recording path on disks and diskettes.

trackball A cursor control device.

translate To move a block of display data to a new position. See also *dragging.*

translucent Admits the passage of light and images; partially transparent.

transmitted light Light which passes through an object or medium. See also *reflected light.*

transparency A monchrome or color positive; the image to be viewed or reproduced by transmitted light.

turnaround time The time required from start to finish to complete a function. See also *throughput.*

turnkey system A complete computer system, usually designed for a specific purpose with selected software.

underlay A registered layer used as background or reference data behind or under another layer. See also *composite; overlay.*

UNIX Operating system developed by Bell Labs.

upgrade Additions to or improvements in a computer system.

user-defined Describing software programming and PROMs which are controlled by the system operator.

utilities Standard or routine software functions.

vacuum frame A vacuum-assisted contact exposure frame. See also *contact frame.*

vellum Translucent drafting material of high quality.

viewing Looking at an image or three-dimensional frame or solid from a set angle.

virtual memory Memory space which is accessible by any capable function.

volitile memory RAM memory which is erased by loss of power.

wash-off A photographic emulsion which is moist-erasable after processing.

wetware Dynamic human brain or gray matter, without which firmware, hardware, and software are useless.

whiteprint A positive diazo-process reproduction producing blue or black lines on a white field.

window A specific polygonal area of the display, usually rectangular.

wire frame Definition of a three-dimensional object by connecting discrete edge points and intersections, thereby defining apparent surfaces and planes.

Winchester disk Generic name for a complete hard-disk system. See also *fixed disk.*

word A text set; also a functional capacity term for computer power stated in bits and bytes (for example, 16 bits, 2 bytes).

word processing Data manipulation of alphanumeric characters as text only; distinct from number crunching, data processing, and graphics processing.

wrong reading See *reverse image.*

X axis Horizontal coordinates reference system.

xerographics Electrostatic process copying; based upon generic use of the name of Xerox Corporation.

Y axis Vertical coordinates reference system.

Z axis Third-axis coordinates reference system.

zero point Generally the lower-left-hand corner of a display window, plot window, or drawing sheet. See also *origin point.*

zoom Enlargement or reduction of display image as an apparent scale change for increased clarity.

References

Books

B1: Anthony Ralston, (ed.), *Encyclopedia of Computer Science and Engineering,* 2d ed., Nostrand Reinhold, Princeton, N.J., 1983.

B2: William S. Davis, *Operating Systems, A Systematic View,* 2d ed. Addison-Wesley, Reading, Mass., 1983.

B3: Timothy H. Merrett, *Relational Information Systems,* Reston Publishing, Reston, Va., 1984.

B4: K. Lonberg-Holm and C. Theodore Larson, *Development Index,* University of Michigan, Ann Arbor, 1953.

B5: William Dudley Hunt, Jr., (ed.), *Comprehensive Architectural Services,* American Institute of Architects, McGraw-Hill, New York, 1965.

B6: Linn C. Stuckenbruck (ed.), *The Implementation of Project Management,* Project Management Institute, Addison-Wesley, Reading, Mass., 1981.

B7: Gary M. Gerlach (ed.), *Pin Graphics Manual,* International Reprographic Association, Franklin Park, Ill., 1980.

B8: Edgar Powers, Jr., *Unigrafs,* Gresham, Smith, Nashville, Tenn., 1980.

B9: Fred A. Stitt, *Systems Drafting,* McGraw-Hill, New York, 1981.

B10: S. Atre, *Data Base: Structured Techniques for Design, Performance and Management,* John Wiley, New York, 1980.

B11: August Strotz, *Recommended Standards on Production Procedures,* Northern California Chapter American Institute of Architects, San Francisco, Calif., 1980.

B12: Bruce A. Artwick, *Applied Concepts in Microcomputer Graphics,* Prentice-Hall, Englewood Cliffs, N.J., 1984.

B13: J. D. Foley and A. Van Dam, *Fundamentals of Interactive Computer Graphics,* Addison-Wesley, Reading, Mass., 1982.

B14: Dan Raker and H. Rice, *Inside AutoCAD,* New Riders Publishing, Thousand Oaks, Calif., 1985.

B15: Thomas French and Carl Svensen, *Mechanical Drawing for High Schools,* McGraw-Hill, New York, 1927.

B16: Hyman H. Katz, *Handbook of Layout and Dimensioning for Production,* Macmillan, New York, 1957.

B17: John Naisbitt, *Megatrends*, Warner Books, New York, N.Y., 1982.

B18: Helen Varley (ed.), *Color*, Marshall Editions Limited, London, 1980.

B19: *Technical Drawings—Lettering—Part 1: Currently Used Characters*, ISO 3089/1-1974(E), International Organization for Standardization, 1974.

B20: *Microcopying—ISO Test Chart No. 2—Descriptions and Use in Photographic Documentary Reproduction*, ISO 3334-1976(E), International Organization for Standardization, 1976.

B21: *Line Conventions and Lettering*, ANSI Y14.2M-1979; American National Standards Institute, Washington, D.C., 1979.

B22: *Standard for the Protection of Records*, NFPA no. 232-1970, National Fire Protection Association, Washington, D.C., 1970.

Articles

A1: Gary M. Gerlach, "Human CADD (aka: Pin Graphics) " *Plan and Print.* Repro/CADD/Systems column, March 1985.

A2: Michael Schley, "CAD Buyer's Checklist," *Architectural Technology*, summer 1985.

A3: "Computer Graphics for Architecture: Techniques in Search of Problems," *Architectural Record*, mid-August 1977.

A4: A. Fujimoto and K. Iwata, "Jag Free Edges on Raster Displays," *IEEE Computer Graphics and Applications*, December 1983.

A5: Gerald Murch, "Physiological Principles for the Effective Use of Color," *IEEE Computer Graphics and Applications*, November 1984.

A6: Gregory MacNicol, "Color Monitor Specmanship: Look before You Leap," *Digital Design*, November 1985.

A7: Jim Kenney, "Careful Color Matching Makes Hardcopy Output Conform to CRT Display," *Computer Technology Review*, fall 1985.

A8: Ken A. Johnson, "CADD Offers Capabilities for Facilities Applications," *Computer Graphics Today*, August 1984.

A9: Maria McCormick and William Wrennall, "A Step beyond Computer Aided Layout," *Industrial Engineering*, May 1985.

A10: Gary M. Gerlach, "Repligraphics," *Plan and Print*, Pin Graphics Hang-Ups column, May 1984.

A11: Gary M. Gerlach, "Top Edge Borderline Confrontation," *Plan and Print*, Pin Graphics Hang-Ups column, January 1981.

A12: "Can Overlay Drafting and Computer-Aided Design Increase Drawing Productivity?" *Kodak Compass*, Drafting Hints column, August 1983.

A13: "Industry Gets Serious about Solid Modeling;" *Computer Aided Engineering*, November-December 1982.

A14: Rida Farouki and John Hinds, "A Hierarchy of Geometric Forms,' *IEEE Computer Graphics and Applications*, May 1985.

A15: Robert Johnson, "Solid Modeling for CAD/CAM," *Computer Graphics World*, November 1982.

A16: "The Solid Modeling Marketplace," *Computer Graphics World*, November 1982.

A17: "Do It Yourself Post Processors for Faster NC Operations," *Computer Aided Engineering*, April 1985.

A18: Gary M. Gerlach, "Backwash: Return to Tomorrow: Color," *Repro Report* Newsletter, Pin Graphics/Reprographics column, June 1983.

A19: Gary M. Gerlach, "Multi-color Reprographics," *Repro Report*, Pin Graphics/Reprographics column, December 1984.

A20: Barbara Meier, 'BUCOLIC: A Program for Teaching Color Theory to Art Students," *IEEE Computer Graphics and Applications*, July 1985.

A21: Gary M. Gerlach, "Interindustry Standards," *Repro Report*, Pin Graphics/Reprographics column, November 1985.

A22: Boyd Jones, "Thermal Ink Transfer," *Computer Graphics World*, May 1984.

A23: Gary M. Gerlach, "Computer Aided Drafting," *Plan and Print*, Repro/CADD/Systems column, February 1985.

A24: Gary M. Gerlach, "Reprographic Services for CADD," *Repro Report*, Pin Graphics/Reprographics column, June 1983.

A25: Gary M. Gerlach, "Production Drafting Techniques: Media," *Plan and Print*, Repro/CADD/Systems column, January 1985.

A26: Gary M. Gerlach, "Display to Plot to Repro," *Plan and Print*, Repro/CADD/Systems column, May 1985.

A27: Gary M. Gerlach, "CADD Hardcopy Output," *Plan and Print*, November 1984.

A28: "Advances in Color Hardcopy Technology," *Computer Graphics World*, January 1984.

A29: Gary M. Gerlach, "Freeing up the Plot Jam," *Plan and Print*, Pin Graphics Hang-Ups column, January 1982.

A30: Gary M. Gerlach, "Hardcopy Output Characteristics," *Repro Report*, Pin Graphics/Reprographics column, October 1984.

A31: Gary M. Gerlach, "CADD Plotter Supplies," *Repro Report*, Pin Graphics/Reprographics column, December 1984.

A32: Gary M. Gerlach, "Contact Reprographics," *Plan and Print*, Pin Graphics Hang-Ups column, April 1980.

A33: Gary M. Gerlach, "Hardcopy Is, Is Not the Master," *Repro Report*, Pin Graphics/Reprographics column, September 1983.

A34: Paul M. Artlip, "Choosing the Right Storage Media Is a Matter of Knowing All the Options," *Design Graphics World*, November 1985.

A35: Richard L. Banks, "Optical Disk Storage and Microfilm Systems Find Separate Applications," *Computer Technology Review*, fall 1985.

A36: David Addleman and Lloyd Addleman. "Rapid 3D Digitizing," *Computer Graphics World*, November 1985.

A37: Andrew Lippman, Walter Bender, Gitta Solomon, and Mituo Saito, "Color Word Processing, *IEEE Computer Graphics and Applications*, June 1985.

A38: Andrew J. Scott, "Integrating Raster and Vector Systems for Mapping," *Computer Graphics World*, February 1984.

A39: Gerald M. Murch, "Perceptual Considerations of Color," *Computer Graphics World*, July 1983.

A40: Morris L. Samit, "The Color Interface," *Computer Graphics World*, July 1983.

A41: Leigh Bellingall, "Trends in Automatic Data Capture," *Computer Graphics World*, September 1985.

A42: *Reprographics (Brochure)*, International Reprographic Association, Franklin Park, Ill., 1982.

A43: Gary M. Gerlach, "On Target," *Repro Report*, Pin Graphics/Reprographics column, May 1986.

A44: Gary M. Gerlach, "From CADD to Pin Graphics and Return," *Plan and Print*, May 1986.

A45: Gary M. Gerlach, "Consistent Post-Punching," *Plan and Print*, Repro/CADD/Systems column, November 1984.

A46: Gary M. Gerlach, "CADD-DO: Re-registering Post-Punching," *Repro Report*, Pin Graphics/Reprographics column, January 1986.

A47: "Chemistry: Useful Buckyballs," *Science Digest*, Newscience column, May 1986.

A48: Marshall Faintich, "Generating Halftone Images for Technical Publishing," *Computer Graphics World*, September 1985.

Seminars and Tutorials

S1: Gary M. Gerlach, *The Transition to CADD*, Computer Graphics '84 Convention, National Computer Graphics Association, Anaheim, Calif., May 1984.

S2: Gary M. Gerlach, *T-7: The Transition to CADD,* BP'84 Convention, NCGA and World Computer Graphics Association, San Francisco, Calif., August 1984.

S3: Gary M. Gerlach, *T-31: Integrating CADD and Reprographics,* A/E Systems Convention, A/E Systems, Inc., Anaheim, Calif., June 1985.

S4: Gary M. Gerlach, *T-11: Integrating CADD and Reprographics,* CMC'85 and A/E Systems Fall Convention, A/E Systems, Inc., Houston, Tex., October 1985.

Index

Acceleration (plot speed), 105–108, 140
Access, 116, 122, 137–138
Acquisition:
    of CADD, 24, 33, 44, 111, 152
        checklist for, 33, 132
    of minimum package, 37–38
    of next system, 41
Algorithm, 15
Alignment, visual, 141, 143
    (*See also* Registration)
Alphanumerics, 11–12, 14, 23, 105, 125–127
Alternative approaches, 131–152
Analog computer, 11–12
ANSI (American National Standards Institute), 96, 99
Antialiasing, 23
Aperture card, 103
Applications software, 35–36, 39
    spreadsheet, 20, 28
    word processing, 10, 20
Archival quality, 102, 113
Artificial intelligence, 2, 38
Attribute, 36, 121
Audit trail, 59, 115, 144

Background, 5, 139, 145
Backlog, 146
Backup, 37, 39, 65
    file, 116–117
    hardcopy master, 113, 116
    incremental, 118
    partial, 118
    softcopy, 116–117
Ballpoint pen, 95, 102, 108
BASIC language, 20
Best-use application, 24, 36, 141–142, 152

Binary digit, 6, 12
Bit, 6, 12
Black line, 110
Blowback, 103–104, 111, 138
Blue line, 110
Bond media, 108
Boolean geometry, 82–83
Bottom line, 152
Break command, 18, 114, 116, 122
Byte, 6, 12

CAD (computer-aided design), 2
CADD (computer-aided design and drafting), 1, 54, 69–70
    acquisition of, 24, 33, 44, 111, 152
    alternatives to, 131–136
    applications of, 3, 31, 33–34, 59, 90–91, 135, 141, 152
    best-way use, 24, 36, 141–142, 152
    conventional systems and, 28–29, 131, 136–141
    electronic drafter, 17, 113
    functions of, 32, 93
    goal of, 138
    hardcopy filing and, 125–126
    housekeeping and, 113–129
    intermittent project effort, 134
    justification for, 24
    layers in, 75–86, 119–120, 141–144, 147–152
    leasing arrangements for, 41
    macroview of I/O, 60–62
    manager for, 41–42, 89
    output (*see* Hardcopy output; Softcopy output)
    pin graphics and, 149 (*see* Pin graphics)
    test procedures for training, 90–91
    transition to, 94, 120, 131, 152

CADD (*Cont.*).
  value added by, 94–95
CADesign, 16, 34, 51, 53, 60, 63, 90, 93
CADrafting, 4, 19, 34, 51, 63, 90, 93–94
CAE (computer-aided engineering), 53–60
CAM (computer-aided manufacturing), 53–60
Cartridge, 22
Cassette, 22, 103
  video, 101–104
CAT (computer-aided testing), 52, 54, 61
Character, 11
Checking file, 122
Checkplot, 21, 22, 70, 102, 108–109, 127, 149
Chip, 20
CIM (computer-integrated manufacturing), 55
Circuit board, 20
Color, 88, 98
Color display, 13, 20, 23, 65, 76–77, 84–88, 93–94, 96–99, 111–112, 129, 149
Color hardcopy, 38, 93, 98–99, 100–105, 151
Color monitor, 23, 39, 88
Color offset, 111
Color transparency, 104
COM (computer-output microfilm), 21, 38, 56–59, 70, 115
Command, 16–17, 75, 83, 89, 125
  break, 18, 114, 116, 122
Compatibility, 38–39, 68, 145
Composite, 114, 140, 148, 151
Computer systems, 1
  minimum, 39
  staged entry into, 39
Consultant, 67–68, 125, 128, 145
  interface, 141
  offline, 128, 145
Contact copy, 71, 138, 140, 148
Continuing education, 41
  (*See also* Training)
Continuous tone, 139
Contract document, 108–110, 114, 131, 150
Contrast, 88, 98
Controller, 16, 20
Coordinates, 11, 14, 77–79, 84, 90
Cost center, 25
Cost control:
  personnel, 25
  project, 24

CPU (central processing unit), 16, 20
Cross hairs, 144, 148
CRT (cathode ray tube), 10, 21, 77, 86, 122
Cursor, 21, 89–91
Cut and tape, 49, 95, 126, 138
Cycle of development, 45

Daisy wheel, 13, 23, 105, 123
Data backup (*see* Backup)
Data integrity, 116, 127
Data processing, 1, 10, 59
  electronic, 1, 11, 59
Data sharing, 145
Database management, 19, 54, 66, 71, 111, 114, 116, 138
  file management and, 120–121, 125, 137
  relational, 19, 55, 120–121, 138–142
Database master, 114
DBMS (database management system), 32, 53, 60, 120–121, 136
Design:
  CADD applications, 35, 135, 142
  phases of, 45–46, 64–66, 114
  process of, 43, 47, 141–142
  program, 20, 45, 65
  scope changes in, 144
De-spooling, 32, 67, 125
  (*See also* Plotters)
Details, plotted, 138–139
Development index, 45
Diazo copying, 146, 148
Diazo emulsion, 108, 138, 141
Difference, 82
Digital computer, 12
Digitizing, 6, 14, 21–22, 49, 74, 76, 89, 118, 128, 140
Dimensional stability, 102, 107, 110, 115, 141, 143, 148
Dimensioning:
  automatic, 19, 91
  conventional, 73–74
  metric, 73–75
Dimensions, 76, 78
  four, 77
  three, 17–19, 81
  two, 17–19, 77
DIP (dual in-line pin) switch, 123
Disciplines, 6, 28–29, 51, 67–68, 71, 76, 84, 120, 150
Disk, 21, 116–117
  fixed, 39–40

Disk (*Cont.*):
  floppy, 39–40, 117, 145
Display:
  color (*see* Color display)
  CRT, 10, 21, 77, 86, 122
  flat-plane, 18, 77, 82
  hardcopy, 146
  high-resolution, 15, 102–103
  interactive, 20–22
  monochrome, 23, 37, 86–87, 93, 152
  raster, 14–15, 88, 97, 102, 111
  sheet size for, 72–75
Documentation (*see* Filing; Hardcopy output-
      put)
DOS (disk operating system), 66
Dot matrix plotter, 39, 105, 123
Dot matrix printer, 13, 23, 40, 102, 105,
      123
Dots per inch, 15
  (*See also* Pixel; Raster plot)
Drafting:
  advanced, 143, 147, 150
  basic, 2
  CADD applications in, 34–35, 90–91,
      139–140
  conventional, 1, 21, 70, 95, 133
  electronic (*see* Electronic drafting)
  film for, 108–110
  layered, 150–151
  manual, 131–134, 137, 142
  mixing CADD with manual, 132, 139–
      144
  photographic, 49, 139
  repligraphic (*see* Repligraphics)
  repro-systems, 4–8, 27, 49, 74–76, 132,
      138–141
  review process in, 2–10, 17, 46, 69–72,
      78, 136–137
Drafting functions, 95
Drawings:
  created on system, 64, 146
  intelligent, 36, 66, 105
  percent on system, 62–64
  set-up rules for, 72–76, 93
  working, 109–112
Duplication, 5, 7, 125
  (*See also* Reproduction)

Editing, 6, 76, 96, 119, 128
  (*See also* Command; Review and revi-
      sion process)
EDP (electronic data processing), 1, 11,
      59

Electron beam recording, 22, 101, 103
Electronic drafting, 2, 14, 17, 71, 80, 89–
      90, 94–97, 100, 113, 138
  (*See also* CADD; Drafting)
Electronic filing, 113, 115–116
Electronic office, 113–114
Electrostatic copying, 146, 148
Electrostatic plotter, 38, 88, 101, 102,
      112, 124, 146
Electrostatic printer, 88, 102, 105
Electrostatics, 95, 106
Emulsion, 103–104, 109, 138
  diazo, 108, 138, 141
  silver halide, 103, 138–141
End point, 90
End result, 24, 86, 152
Enlargement, 110, 111
Erasability, 110, 146
Erasure, 95, 114
Error, 18, 109, 114, 116, 122, 128
Escape command, 18, 114, 116, 122
Exposure, 103

Face, 81
Facilities management, 55
Felt-tip (fiber-tip) marker, 94–95, 97,
      102, 107
Fiducial, 142–143, 148
Field fill, 98
Filing, 53–56, 95, 113, 139, 147
  electronic, 113, 115–116
  hardcopy, 108–109, 113–115, 122–129
  indirect, 122
  layered, 8–10, 118–121, 146, 148
  plot (*see* Plot file)
  softcopy, 114–118, 125
  (*See also* Database management;
      DBMS)
Film, polyester, 102, 107, 110, 115, 141,
      143, 148
Financing, 24, 25
Finite element analysis, 19, 54, 78, 84,
      102, 126
Firmware, 19–20, 78
  (*See also* Hardware)
Fixed disk, 39–40
Flag, 36, 121
Flat plane, 18, 77, 82
Floppy disk, 39–40, 117, 145
Format, 91, 110–111
  drawing, 72, 136, 143–144
  plotting, 109–111, 136, 146

Geodesic dome, 91
Ghost, 71, 79, 86, 151–152
Graphics:
  business, 13
  color alternatives for, 98
  interactive, 10, 20, 70–71, 101, 122,
    128
  laser, 115
  output systems for, 23
  pin (*see* Pin graphics)
  three-dimensional, 17, 40, 53, 77, 81–
    82, 91
  two-dimensional, 18, 39, 76–79
Graphics logic, 13–14
Graphite:
  drafting lead, 95
  toner, 102, 105

Halftone, 139
Handshake, 37, 123
Hard disk, 39–40
Hardcopy output, 5–8, 21–23, 36–37, 56,
    59, 84, 86, 92–97, 100–111, 127,
    132, 141, 146
  decision tree for, 101
  drafting for, 35, 93–94
  for filing, 108–109, 113–115, 122–
    129
  master, 113, 114, 116, 125
  offline, 104, 114, 122–125, 141–145
  photographic, 103–104
  plotted, 70–71, 100–105, 136, 141–145,
    147–149
  reproduction of, 108, 136
  revisions to, 127, 129
  three-dimensional, 18, 129
Hardware, 15–16, 35–36
  minimum, 20–21, 34
  (*See also* Firmware)
Hatching, 91, 98
Head:
  laser, 103, 104
  optical, 104
  plotter, 143
  printer, 13, 105, 123
Hidden line, 79, 81–83
Hidden surface, 78–80
High resolution, 15, 102–103
Housekeeping, 113–129
Human-cadd, 9, 150

Icon, 89

Image, 2–4, 9, 13–15, 18
  projection, 103–104, 111, 139
  reverse, 109–110
  right, 108
  subordinate, 71
  translucent, 72, 103, 111
Imaging (*see* Display; Hardcopy output;
    Image)
Imperial sheet size, 73–74
In-fill, 91, 98
Ink-jet plotter, 40, 88, 97, 102, 112
Ink-jet printer, 40, 88, 102, 105
Input, 44, 70, 89, 92, 141
Instruction, 75, 83, 89, 125
Intelligent drawing, 36, 66, 105
Intelligent line, 19, 121
Intelligent text, 19, 121
Interactive display, 20–22
Interactive graphics, 10, 20, 70–71, 101,
    122, 128
Interactive system, 22
Interface, operator-machine, 88–91
Interface consultant, 141
Intermediate, 110, 145
Intermediate checking file, 122
International Reprographic Association,
    85–86
Interpreter, 16, 20
I/O (input/output), 44, 62
  (*See also* Input; Output)
Isometric view, 78–81

Jaggies, 15
Joystick, 23, 39, 89
Justification for a CADD system, 24

Key operator, 41–42, 89
Keyboard, 21, 39, 89

Laser graphics, 115
Laser plotter, 88, 103, 111, 112, 124, 148,
    152
Laser printer, 88, 104
Layers:
  conventions for, 18, 75–79, 90–91, 140–
    141
  differentiated, 149–151
  filing, 118–121, 146, 148
  layered systems, 8–10, 118–121, 146,
    148
  logic control, 54, 69–91

Layers (*Cont.*):
  plotting, 147–150
  registered, 8–11, 111, 141–144, 147–
    149, 152
  revision, 128–129
  surfaces, 78–81
  target template and, 144
Leasing, 41
Letter-quality printer, 105
Library, 138
Light pen, 21, 89
Lines:
  checklist for creating, 17–18
  hidden, 79, 81–83
  intelligent, 19, 121
  phantom, 79
  types of, 90–91, 95–97, 133, 150
Liquid ink, 95, 97, 105–107
Lithography, 87, 111
Logic:
  data, 11–13
  graphics, 13–15
Logical pen, 77, 96–97, 150
Loop, 7, 72

Machine code, 20
Macro, 37, 89, 100, 125
  (*See also* Command; Software)
Macroview of I/O, 60–62
Magnetic tape, 36, 103–104
Mainframe, 38
Maintenance:
  master file, 113
  plot file, 113, 122–123
  system, 146
Manual drafting, 131–134, 137, 142
Mass storage (*see* Fixed disk)
Master drawing, 113
Master file, 113–114
Matte, 108, 111, 139, 142
Media, 104–108, 148
Memory, 21–22
  volatile, 105, 114–115
  (*See also* CPU; Filing; Fixed disk;
    RAM; ROM)
Menu, 21, 89
Metric sheet size, 73–75
Microcomputer, 11, 38, 139
Microfiche, 103
Microfilm, 38, 56, 103
Micrographics, 56, 71, 95, 103, 115, 146
  COM, 21, 38, 56–59, 70, 115
Microprocessor, 16, 20

Minicomputer, 11, 16, 38, 139
Mirror, 18
Modeling, 82–84
Modem, 21, 38, 145
Monitor, 23, 39, 77
  RGB, 88
  (*See also* CRT; Display)
Monochrome display, 23, 37, 86–87, 93,
  152
Mouse, 21, 39, 89
MRP (material resource planning), 55, 61
Mylar, 70 (*see* Polyester film)

Negative, 103, 110–111, 114, 148–152
Network, 7, 68, 125, 145
Nonreproducible copy, 108, 111
Number crunching, 11
Numerical control, 18, 46–48, 55, 72, 84,
  103
  (*See also* Robotics)

Off-stream, 134, 141–142
Offline consultant, 128, 145
Offline hardcopy, 104, 114, 122–125,
  141–145
Offset, 87, 111
On-stream, 134
Online copy, 122–125, 137
OOPS! command, 18, 114, 116, 122
Opaque copy, 108, 111
Operating systems, 42
  DOS, 66
  MS-DOS, 39
  UNIX, 39
Operator error, 109, 116, 121–122
Operator training, 37, 41–42, 67–68, 90,
  92, 152
Optical reticle, 143
Origin point, 79–80, 143
Original, 113
  master, 113
  trashed, 95, 109
  workable, 102, 104, 111, 139, 141
Orthographic view, 66, 79
Output, 44, 70, 92, 151–152
  action list for, 38
  display of, 23, 89, 93
  electronic, 121
  filing of (*see* Filing)
  hardcopy (*see* Hardcopy output)
  softcopy (*see* Softcopy output)
  usable, 132, 141–142, 150
  workable, 1, 105–106, 108, 111, 141

Overlay:
   control, 69
   drafting, 49–51, 95, 114, 141–144
   plotted, 139–141, 145–151

Pan, 18
Password, 37, 42
Paste-up, 49
Pen:
   light, 21, 89
   logical, 77, 96–97, 150
   physical, 77, 96–97, 150
   (*See also* Plotters)
Peripheral, 20, 36
Permanent damage, 18, 116, 121–122
Personnel:
   cost of, 28
   training of, 41–42, 67
Phantom line, 79
Phantom program, 118
Photodrafting, 49, 139–140
Photographic hardcopy, 103–104
Photoplotter, 97, 103–104, 111
Photoprojection, 103–104, 111, 138
Photorestoration, 5, 49, 110, 111, 147
Physical pen, 77, 96–97, 150
Pin graphics, 8, 49, 70–71, 76, 80, 94–95,
   114, 119, 144, 148
Pinbar, 143, 147
Pixel, 14, 139
Plastic lead, 95
Plot configuration, 124–125
Plot file, 67, 108, 114, 122, 137, 146–150
   maintenance of, 113, 122–123
   protocols, 124
Plot flow, 147
Plot jam, 146
Plot registration, 141–149
Plot spool, 67, 109, 122–125, 137
Plot time, 146–149
Plots:
   black line, 110
   blue line, 110
   quick-look, 21, 22, 70, 102, 108–109,
      127, 149
   raster, 14–15, 88, 97, 102, 111
   thermographic, 21–22, 70, 102
   vector, 15, 88, 97, 102, 107, 124, 134,
      143
Plotters:

Plotters (*Cont.*):
   beltbed, 143, 147
   controller handshake for, 123
   dot matrix, 39, 123
   drum-type, 143, 147
   electrostatic, 38, 88, 101, 102, 112, 124,
      146
   flatbed, 143, 147
   formats and, 109–111
   graphics output and, 95–99
   grit-wheel, 142
   ink-jet, 40, 88, 97, 102, 112
   laser, 88, 103, 111, 112, 124, 148, 152
   multipen, 39, 97, 150
   multiple copying and, 109
   photo, 97, 103–104, 111
Polyester film, 102, 107, 110, 115, 141,
   143, 148
Polygon fill, 98
Positive, 49, 102, 138, 148
Post-punching, 143–144, 148
Presentation, 65, 93, 103
Primary memory, 37, 39, 116
   (*See also* Backup)
Print, 110
Printed circuit, 54
Printed format, 74
Printers:
   daisy wheel, 13, 23, 105, 123
   dot matrix, 13, 23, 40, 102, 105, 123
   electrostatic, 88, 102, 105
   ink-jet, 40, 88, 102, 105
   laser, 88, 104
   letter-quality, 105
   protocols for, 124
   thermographic, 21, 71, 102
Probe, 23, 89
   electromagnetic, 4
Process:
   camera, 104, 111
   color, 88, 98
   photonegative, 148
Production:
   drafting, 69, 92
   equipment (*see* Hardcopy output;
      Workstation)
   workhours, 28–31
Productivity, 27, 30–31, 62, 72, 81, 92,
   94, 137, 149
Program design, 20, 45, 65
   (*See also* Software)
Projection image, 103–104, 111, 139
Projects:

Projects (*Cont.*):
  management of, 134
  phases of, 45–49
  team approach to, 68, 141
PROM (programmable read-only memory), 20
Puck, 21, 39, 89

Qualified vendor, 33
Quality output, 93, 104, 109, 111
Quantity take-offs, 32–33
Questions, primary, 26–27
Quick-look plot, 21, 22, 70, 102, 108–109, 127, 149

RAM (random-access memory), 37, 39, 116
Raster plot, 14–15, 88, 97, 102, 111
Record keeping, 113–129
  (*See also* Filing)
Records:
  important, 115, 126
  nonessential, 115, 127
  useful, 115, 126
  vital, 115, 125
Reduction, 111
Reduction-enlargement factor, 111
Registration, 8–11, 32, 111, 119, 141–144, 147–149, 152
  plot, 141–149
Relational database management, 19, 55, 120–121, 138–142
Repligraphics, 9, 51, 56, 94, 110–111, 114, 133, 145–146, 149–152
Replotting, 95, 109, 136, 146, 151
Reproduction:
  cost of, 94
  final, 69
  hardcopy (*see* Hardcopy output)
  vehicle for, 93
Reprographics, 49, 110–112, 115, 149
  integrated, 37, 131–132
  (*See also* Micrographics)
Reprosystems drafting, 4–8, 27, 74–76, 132, 138–141
Resolution, 15, 97, 102–103
  high, 15, 102–103
  (*See also* Display)
Restoration, 5, 49, 110–111, 115, 138
Return on investment, 26–30, 43, 59, 93
Reverse image, 109–110

Review and revision process, 2–10, 17, 46, 69–72, 78, 136–137
RGB (red-green-blue) monitor, 88
Right image, 108
Robotics, 55, 72, 84
Roller ball, 21, 89
ROM (read-only memory), 19–20
Rotation, 18, 90–91

Scale, 6, 90–91
Scanning, 129
  (*See also* Digitizing)
Scissor-drafting, 49
Screen:
  display, 10, 21, 39, 77, 86, 122
  monitor, 23, 39, 77, 88
Screen tint, 71, 86, 151–152
Scribing, 101–102
Sectioning, 91
Security, 37, 42
  (*See also* Access)
Sepia, 110, 145
Service bureau, 33, 37, 40–41, 67, 146
Shared data elements, 31, 119–121
Sheet:
  format of, 72–75
  plotted, 110, 144, 147–149, 150
  recall of, 121
  size of, 72–75
Silver halide emulsion, 103, 138–141
Sketching, 16, 95
Slicks, 119, 145
Softcopy output, 21, 37–38, 55, 93, 100–101, 103, 113, 115–116
  filing of, 114–118, 125
  systems, 38
Software, 15–20, 38
  applications, 35–36, 39
  commands, 16–17, 89
  database management (*see* Database management)
  four-dimension, 76–77
  line and text configuration, 149–152
  minimum, 15–18
  plotter controller, 122–124
  programming, 72, 82–83
  test procedure for, 90–91
  three-dimension, 18, 40, 77, 91
  two-dimension, 18, 38, 77
  working master, 118
Solids modeling, 82–84
Spatial section, 79

Spline, 14
Spool, plot, 67, 109, 122–125, 137
Spreadsheet software, 20, 28
Stairstepping, 15
Stamp, 95
Stand-alone workstation, 40
Standards, 88, 96, 99–100, 111, 133
Startpoint, 90
Stick-on, 95
Storage, 116–121
    (*See also* Backup; Filing, Housekeep-
        ing; Memory)
Subordinate imaging, 71
Surfaces:
    hidden, 78–81
    modeling of, 82–84
Symbols, 91, 143
Systems:
    drafting, 94
    minimum CADD, 38–39
    mixing of, 141
    upgrading, 40

Tablet (*see* Digitizing; Menu)
Tape:
    drafting, 95, 133
    electromagnetic, 22, 104, 115
    video, 101–104
Target, 144, 148
    (*See also* Registration)
Target template, 144
Tasks:
    design of, 34–35
    drafting, 1, 35
Terminal, 10, 21, 39, 77, 86, 88, 122
    (*See also* CRT; Monitor)
Text:
    checklist for creating, 17–18
    fonts for, 100, 133
    intelligent, 19, 121
    layers of, 76
    types of, 91, 96, 99–100, 149
Thermographic plot, 21–22, 70, 102
    (*See also* Quick-look plot)
Thermographic printer, 21, 71, 102
Three-dimensional graphics, 17, 40, 53,
        77, 81–82, 91
Throughput, 141
Throwaway, 119
Thumb wheel, 21, 39, 89
Timesharing, 33, 37, 40–41, 67, 146
Trace (*see* Display)
Tracing, 66
    (*See also* Drawing)

Track ball, 21, 89
Training, 37, 41–42, 67–68, 90, 92, 152
    personnel, 41–42
    test procedures for, 90–91
Transition to CADD, 94, 120, 131, 152
Translation, 20
Translucent image, 72, 103, 111
Tweaking, 83
Two-dimensional graphics, 18, 39, 76–79

Underlay (*see* Overlay)
Union, 82
UNIX, 39
Upgrade, 40
User defined features, 72
Utilities (*see* Command; Software)

Value added by CADD, 94–95
Variational geometry, 19
Vector plot, 15, 88, 97, 102, 107, 124,
        134, 143
Vellum, 106–108, 110, 115
Video cassette, 101–104
Video tape, 101–104
Viewing (*see* Display)
Volatile memory, 105, 114–115

Wash-off film, 110–111
Wetware, 9, 92
Whiteprint, 110
Winchester disk, 39–40
Window, 18
Wire frame, 53, 81, 83, 91
Word processing, 10, 20
Workable original, 102, 104, 111, 139,
        141
Workable output, 1, 105–106, 108, 111,
        141
Working drawing, 109–112
    (*See also* Contract document)
Workstation, 18, 25, 39, 132, 144
    configuration of, 100
    stand-alone, 40
Wrong reading, 109–110

X axis, 17, 79–82, 103
Xerography, 109, 146, 148

Y axis, 17, 79–82, 103

Z axis, 17, 79–82, 103
Zero point, 79–80, 143
Zoom, 18, 90

ABOUT THE AUTHOR

Gary M. Gerlach, A.I.A., a graduate of the University of Michigan, is a licensed architect in several states with extensive experience in computer applications and project production management. For the past 10 years he has worked as a consultant to architects, engineers, and the reprographics industry on drafting, reprographics, and computer-aided design and drafting (CADD) systems. Now a principal in his own company, Pin Graphic Advisor, Mr. Gerlach conducts in-house training programs, private transition to CADD management programs, and seminars and workshops. He is also the author of many columns and articles on repro/systems drafting, overlay drafting, and CADD applications.